AF412376

Danny Venlet

interior architect & designer

edited by Max Borka

stichting kunstboek

SHOWER, 2006 – "I was born in Australia, from Dutch parents. I studied in Brussels, Belgium, returned to Australia to establish myself as an interior architect and designer, and finally came back to Brussels where I have been living and working until now. Belgium and Australia are opposites, not only from a geographical point of view, but also in many other aspects. Australia is huge and empty, Belgium tiny and crowded. Australia is sunny, Belgium rainy and cloudy. This difference in climate seems to have had its influence on the mentality; Australians are much more generous, relaxed and open, while Belgians have other qualities, such as a unique sense of humour and the surreal. The fact that I am an offspring of both worlds is seen by many as the main explanation for my urge to turn things upside down, or inside out. The *Shower*, which I designed for Viteo, is often quoted as the best example of this topsy-turvydom as it reinvents the shower experience. People often overlook the fact that, just like most of my other designs, the *Shower* mainly results from a very logical and practical thinking; in this case the fact that the standard garden hose that provides the water is lying on the ground. It would be a waste to divert the water upwards before using it. That goes against my philosophy, which is to strive for a maximum effect with a minimum of means. Moreover, most showers that conduct water upwards have the habit of standing askew, which does not look really nice. When people step on the white round base which – apart from the hose – is the only element of this shower, the body of the user immediately activates a mechanism that produces a great number of fine soft water jets that come from little holes along the periphery of this platform. The jets can reach up to 4 m high – depending on the weight of the user – before falling gently down towards the middle. The result is something halfway between a fountain, a water column and a gentle summer rain. It is an extremely sensual experience and was never intended as an alternative to an indoor shower, but rather as a tool for refreshment, to rinse off the sweat and dirt near the pool, in the garden or on a jetty or patio. Inspiration came by observing typical outdoor activities, such as children jumping on boulders, or in puddles. What I particularly like about the *Shower* is that from a minimalist point of view, it is probably my best and purest design, and therefore paradoxically is almost reduced to a non-design as it nearly becomes invisible."

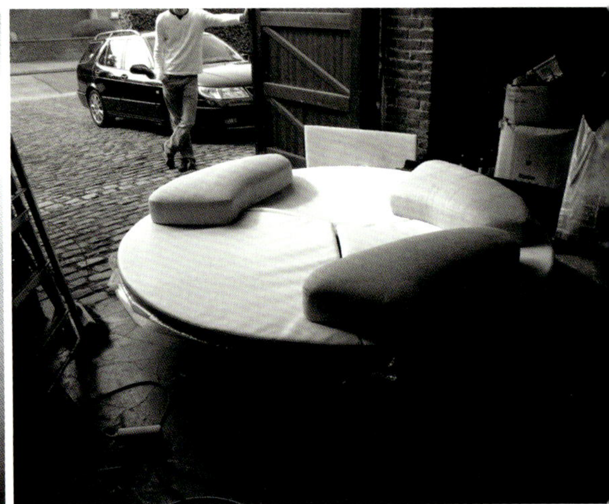

LYLO, 2007 – "Minimalism is almost exclusively associated with straight lines and angles. I've never understood this, and certainly not the dogma that says that curvy lines cannot be used. Look at an egg: isn't that the most perfect minimal form? My minimalism is essentially a curvy one, organic, natural and welcoming, not intimidating. The lines are dynamic, not static. The idea of inciting movement always stood central in my designs. When Viteo asked me to do a bed, I went for a waterbed that can be used indoors as well as outdoors. The form of its white polyester base was inspired by one of the most simple and familiar water containers one can imagine: a soup plate. The inner section has a layer of foamed plastic at the bottom, covered with a bag that is filled with water, and on top of that there's a 5 cm thick overlay made from outdoor imitation leather. This overlay consists of three triangles that are equal in size and form a circle. The paradox here is that the bed gives you the feeling of being on an island, away from the maddening crowd whilst bobbing up and down the calm waters of a deep blue sea, but instead the water is inside the island and not surrounding it."

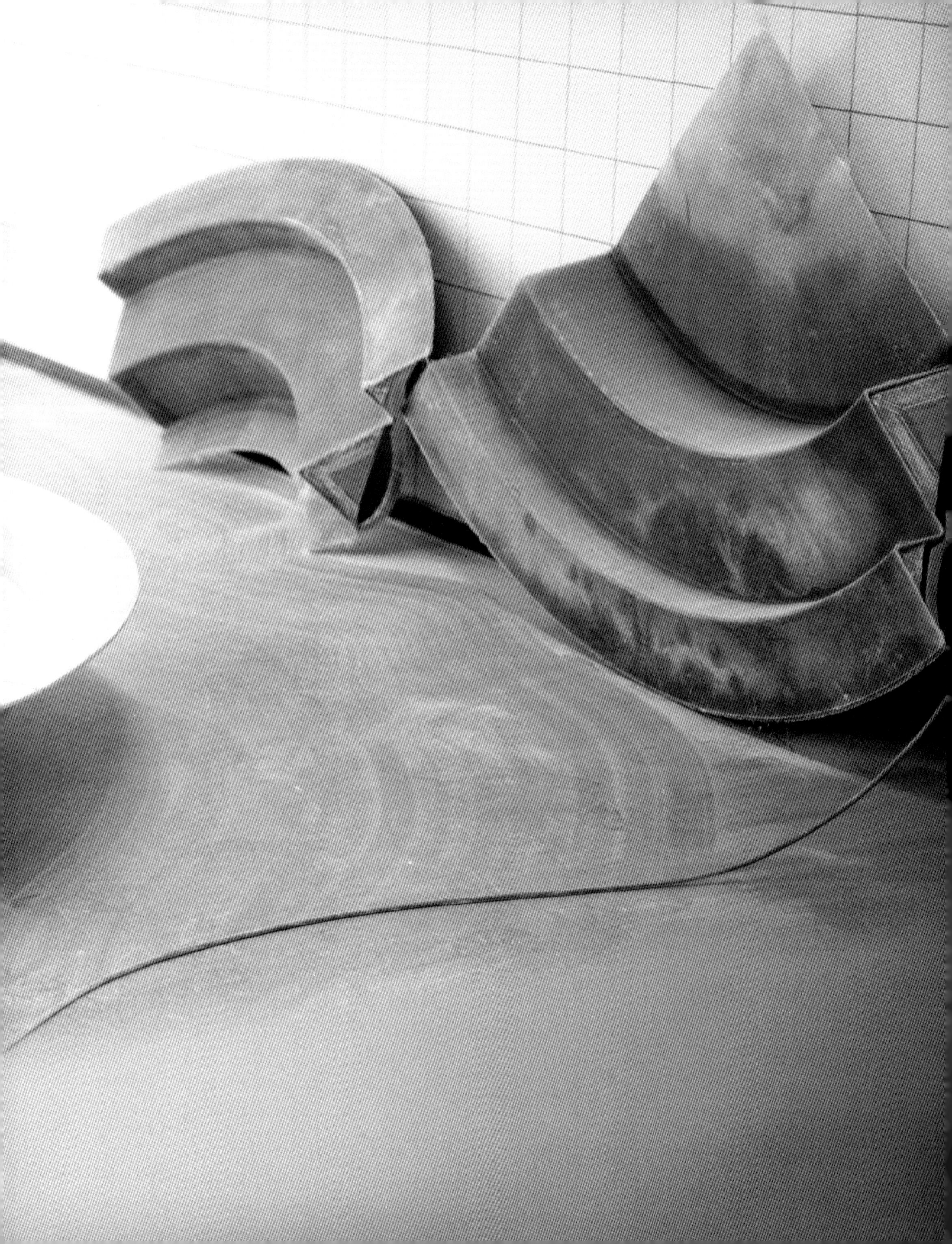

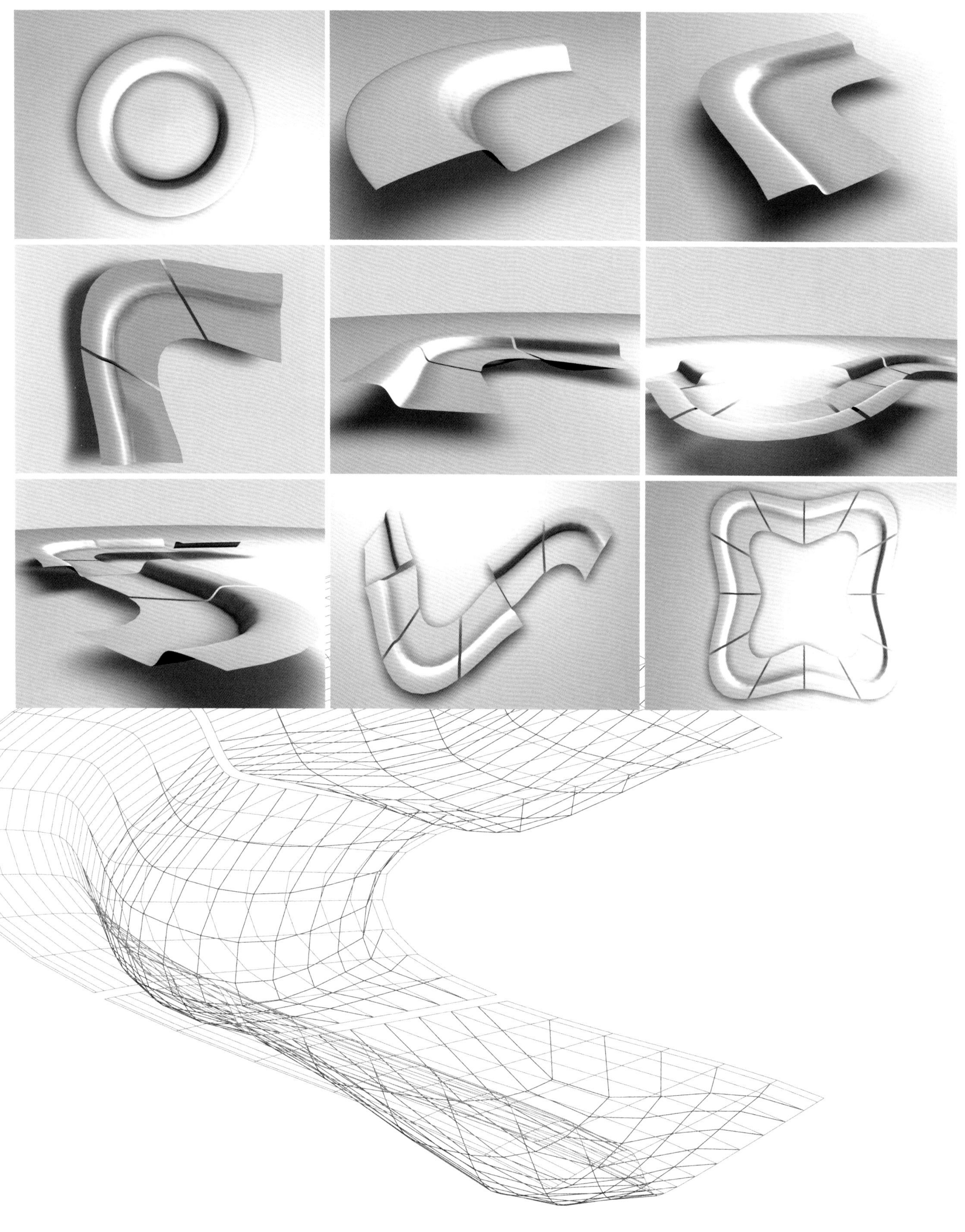

DISH, 2005 – "A good dish needs to be extremely abstract and neutral as a support, and yet it should also be very comforting. It is probably the circular form most familiar to people. I therefore took it as the basis for the design of this sofa. We broke the dish into pieces and recycled and reworked the fragments on the computer till we ended up with something that looked like a flying saucer. For the naked eye, the first impression is that of a futuristic sofa that hovers effortlessly in the air, no longer under the influence of gravity. With a second glance comes a second surprise: the sofa only seems to be kept in a precarious balance by the three hemispheres that form the basis, while hardly touching the ground. The truth behind it is as simple as the proverbial egg of Columbus: the hemispheres have been slightly smoothed underneath, so that the sofa sits on an even surface and a strong and stable support. Everything about the *Dish* is curvy, and working with the hemispheres also had a practical reason: it gave me the possibility to fill them with foam, offering the deep seating surface a comfort that is beyond comparison. But the fact that it is a giant 3D trompe l'oeil is probably its greatest trump."

BENDYBAY, *2007* – *"Similar to the Dish sofa, I developed for the Viteo>Outdoors range a modular sofa-system, consisting of three elements that can be combined into a sequence of wide and sharp or slow and fast turns or bends, freely to be defined by the user, and undulating like a coastline. Hence also its name: BendyBay. Different from the Dish, it rests on legs in stainless steel that support the plastic mould, holding an inner volume in foam. Again, the BendyBay is weatherproof. It is said that I revolutionized outdoor furniture. It probably simply comes from my Australian background: I like to create the possibility to live outdoors as if you were indoors."*

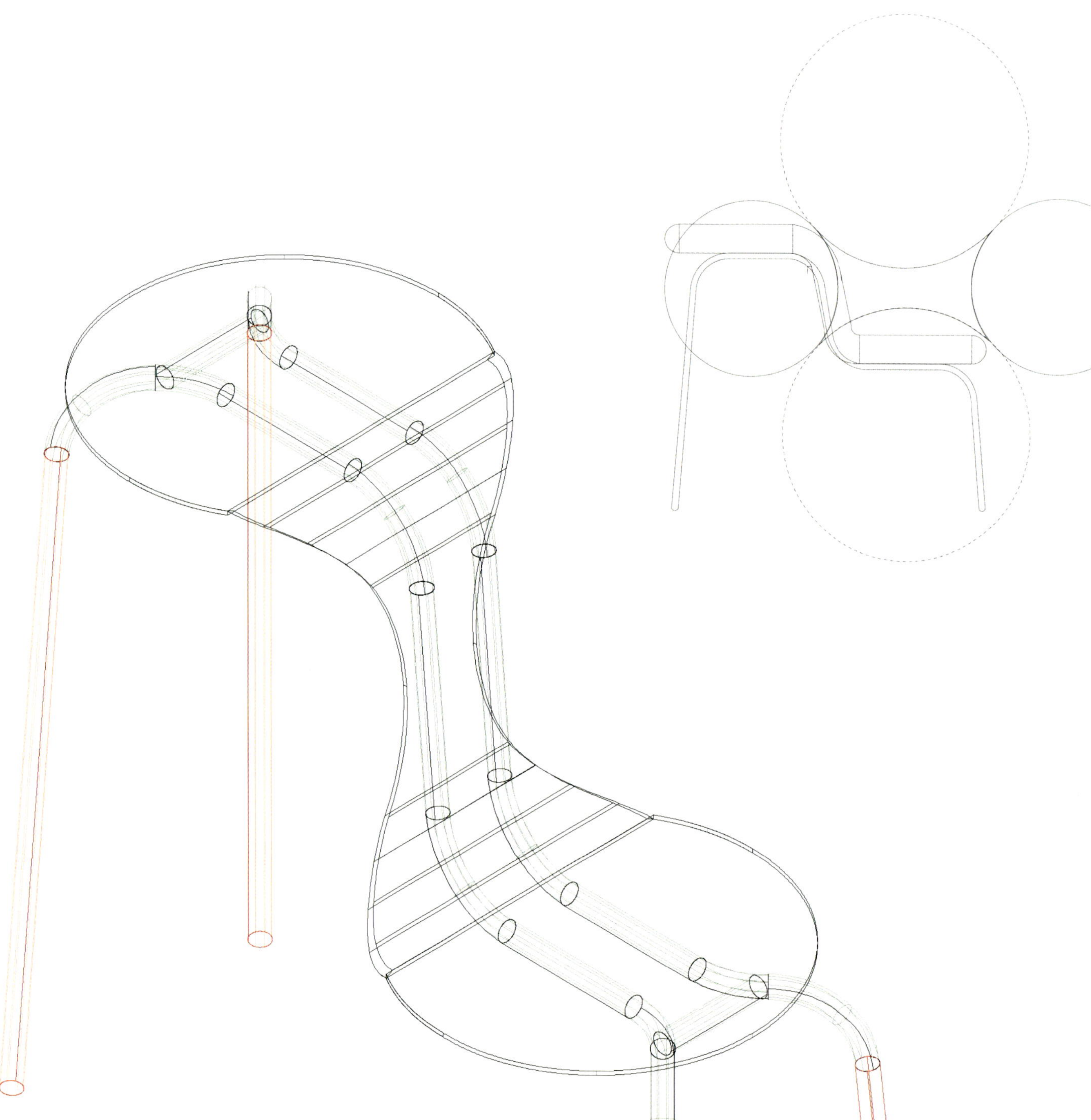

MAN-CHI, 2000 – "I never felt the urge to design a chair on four legs. The *Man-Chi* chair is the only exception. Still, people have to sit on it in the back to front position, in reverse. Most of my early furniture pieces were born out of a specific interior project, in function of a particular space and situation. Although the *Man-Chi* chair later proved to be suitable for a range of other domestic or commercial applications, the initial idea was to develop a massage tool for the *Man-Chi*, a new relaxation centre in Antwerp, Belgium. Most massage chairs look horrible, extremely high-tech, probably to make a link with the seriousness of the medical world. I never understood how anyone could lie down on them and relax. That's why I opted for this simple chair on four legs in stainless steel, and since this 'new urban health centre' almost exclusively focused on men, adapted it to a position men love to take on a chair: back to front, because of the comfort, using their crossed arms as a headrest. By integrating the seat and the back in one single curvaceous and seamless form, upholstered in imitation leather, the *Man-Chi* creates a more organic support for that pose, which is also the most convenient for a massage. The *Man-Chi* directly inspired the *Easy Rider*, which would become my biggest success."

MAN-CHI, relaxation centre for men, 2000, Antwerp, Belgium "While I would later design a shower where the water comes from underneath, the *Man-Chi* relaxation centre has a shower tube for power massage which has to be entered from above by using a small ladder. People see it as a typical Venlet intervention because of its position and cylindrical form. But sometimes the circumstances lend you a helping hand as originally the shower was not planned. Even its form was more the result of necessity and luck. In this case, as we were excavating to increase the ceiling height, we discovered a disused well in the basement. It was abnormally wide in diameter, 122 cm, so we decided to turn that deep hole into a power shower tube in the hammam. *Man-Chi* – which stands for Man-Health – is located in the heart of an up and coming fashion district in Antwerp, and the project evolved as the work progressed. What began as a small shop refurbishment of 50 sq m ended up as my first comprehensive project since my return from Australia, totalling 170 sq m. *Man-chi* relaxation centre now consists of four different areas. With its glass façade the small shop and lobby in front serve as a window display where everything is on show; even one of the *Man-Chi* chairs is strategically fixed to the wall, rotating at night. In this space, which doubles as a waiting room, one can also get a 'quick over the clothes' massage on one of the chairs. The rear space and basement that only became available much later, breathe a more Japanese Zen atmosphere, with three afrormosia wooden cubicle boxes aligned in the back. This is where men can enjoy in silent privacy a massage or foot reflexology. There is even a separate oriental shiatsu massage room. The presence of high design retail outlets in the surrounding area may partly explain why I opted for square forms and a more restrained style devoid of the curves and organic forms found in my earlier works. The simplicity and minimalism of each space and a judicious mix of materials, which is welcoming rather than intimidating, are designed to enhance the sense of serenity. There is an evolution from light to dark in the materials and colours used as you progress. The white walls of the shop and its brightly coloured furniture contrast to the deep natural tones of the afrormosia timber veneer applied to the exterior of the boxes at the back. The floor surface runs from cream epoxy to polished concrete and natural bluestone. The wet spa room in the cellar is entirely made out of black concrete stone, instilling a calming darkness. Since the rear and the basement are a male-only zone, several masculine elements were injected in the interior. Inside the cubicles, that refer to crates, the walls are upholstered with the female side of Velcro, resembling a contemporary toolbox or well-organized garage, to hold anything from towels to massage oil."

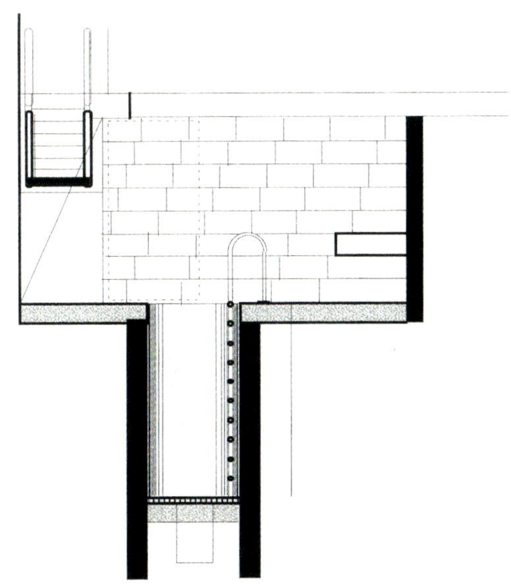

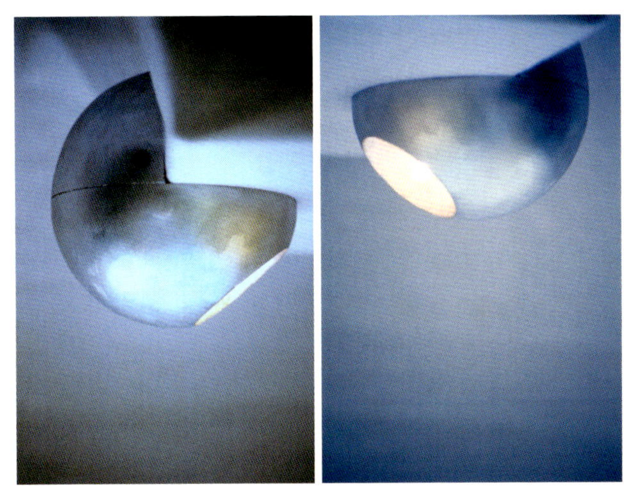

DEDECE, furniture showrooms, 1990/1991, Auckland, New Zealand, Melbourne & Brisbane, Australia – "*DéDéCé* originally stood for Danish Design Centre. But because other non-Danish products became part of the collection, the name was changed. Still, when we were asked to create several showrooms for this Australian furniture dealer, first in Melbourne, then Brisbane and later in Auckland, New Zealand, we were asked to develop a style that would still be close to that of the leader of Danish design, Arne Jacobsen. At that time I was working with Marc Newson, who was a jeweller by education, and Tina Engelen with whom I had started a partnership, called Daffodil design. Marc had been commissioned to do the interior of a clothes shop, Andoni, and had called for my help since he had never done an interior before. The Melbourne showroom was located in a big warehouse, an industrial shoebox-shaped space. To contrast this rectangular shape we created a huge fluid cavity in one of the inner sidewalls, which was clearly visible from the street, by echoing the predominant organic shapes of Jacobsen. The difference in level between the front and the back was bridged by very long steps, offering space for separate displays. A pierced light well in the ceiling with a diameter of 1,8 m and crowned by a flaming rail was designed to tempt visitors to walk to the very end whilst offering a glimpse of the showroom upstairs. Behind the curvy niche, that served as a display for chairs, a staircase led to the first floor where other openings in the ceiling mirrored the one on the ground floor. A crisscross of wooden walls had been grafted on these holes, thus creating different displays that didn't interfere too much with each other. The most characteristic elements of the Melbourne showroom were subsequently used in the showrooms of Brisbane and Auckland – by way of corporate identity."

HATSHOE, hat and shoe shop, 2003, Brussels, Belgium – "Interior design is about respect for the identity of the building, its soul, which is often largely defined by its past. When my Brussels friend and colleague, Dirk Meylaerts and I were asked to refurbish this minuscule hat and shoe shop in the most fashionable street of downtown Brussels, the rue Dansaert, we decided to leave the original art deco interior untouched. We only added a series of shelves that swing like a loop along the walls and the window. They serve as a display and lighting source while leaving plenty of space in the middle and making the 10 sq m shop look even larger than it actually is."

FRAGMA, fashion shop, 2001, Antwerp, Belgium — "I've always liked to wrong-foot people, making them question themselves. A rather modern and inconspicuous corner house that was originally meant for offices had to be transformed into a boutique for men and women. It was situated in the heart of the Antwerp fashion district facing the ModeMuseum and close to the even more famous and sumptuous Modepaleis of Dries van Noten. I humbly opted for an overall approach that was sober and clean, while adding some specially designed warmer elements, such as the luminous seat on the ground floor in the men's section. A long, sensual and elegant banquette was added upstairs where the women's collections were sold. An oversized and minimalist staircase was the biggest eye catcher, connecting both floors and inviting the visitors to go upstairs. It also held an element of surprise as the lower half merged into the top of the counter, obliging people to make a 180° turn if they didn't want to parade the catwalk. One arm of the V shaped space upstairs was divided into small timber boxes that seemed to float because they were illuminated from underneath. Once inside, I wanted to give women the impression to be in a personal wardrobe and therefore each separate little niche contained a different style of woman's wear. Contrasting those little niches was the giant upholstered leather banquette which dominated the second arm of the V, creating a lounge atmosphere where women could try on the clothes and discuss with their friends."

ASHLEY BARBER, photographer's studio, 1991, Newtown, Australia – "This was still a Daffodil project. The rectangular space of a former meat-processing factory was organized along an open plan, while the different functions were grouped around three elements, the highest being a floating circular mezzanine perched on the ceiling trusses. Immediately below, a jewel-like box structure contained the dark room, bathroom and stairs that lead to the mezzanine. A pierced light well in the ceiling functioned as a natural light source for photography during the day. White and wood dominated the space. Since the studio was often used for food photography it needed a well-equipped kitchen. We located it on the outside wall of the box and kept it very open and simple, concealing all appliances under a counter of black-bear veneer. We also lit it with a wash of down-lights. The third element – a giant white backdrop – united the space in one single sweeping curve reaching from the floor to the ceiling. Later, the flexibility of the design was confirmed when the studio was converted into the Sarah Cotter Gallery, almost without any transformation works."

DEWISPELAERE, residence, 2000-2007, Herne, Belgium – "This old farmhouse has a typical long, rectangular ground floor plan with the living space in the middle and stables at both ends. We tried to save as many original elements as possible while expanding the living space to the left. Since the first floor of such a traditional Belgian farmhouse is little more than an attic, hidden under a saddle roof, we enhanced that secret room effect by creating a hidden staircase leading to both the first floor and the cellar. It was installed behind what looked like a cupboard door in the kitchen, which also connects the old and the new part of the ground floor. In order to make everything fit within the bathroom space and leave the beautiful wooden beam structure untouched, we created a central piece that includes a bathtub, toilet and two washbasins."

MAULES, residence, 1991, Annandale, Australia (left)/ MACGOWAN, residence, 1991, Woolloomooloo, Australia (right) – "Respect comes first when we do an interior renovation; playfulness comes second. It explains the great variation in our interior projects. When we were asked to transform a neo-Egyptian heritage building in Annandale in the Maules residence, the building had to be left intact. The only freedom we had left was in the parts that had originally not been there, the kitchen and the bathroom. We gladly accepted and created a sunken bath, totally in line with the Egyptian atmosphere. We even installed an Egyptian style washbasin, and combined it with a sculptural container for towels. The refurbishment of a large old terrace house, originally dating from the 1880s, into the MacGowan residence, also involved the construction of new kitchen and bathroom facilities. While the kitchen was one of deliberate contrasts, the bathroom went for an opposite effect. The luxury in the bathroom lies in the fact that the available space was so enormous that it allowed me to split it in two mirroring halves and double everything. The bright white scheme features two baths and two basins by Luigi Collani and an enormous shower in the middle. The sweeping curve of the drain groove that was necessary to collect water from the open shower, makes the connection between the two symmetrical spaces and reflects the tail of the two seal-shaped antique waterspouts. I even wanted to install two toilets, opposite one other, but my client thought that a bit weird, so I compromised and changed one for a bidet."

BRAAF, residence, 2004, Boom, Belgium – "The client, Renato Braaf , was managing director of Timberland Benelux, the outdoor specialist for whom I had refurbished a new showroom/headquarters in Aartselaar. The loft, situated in a former mill, was totally empty apart from the supporting pillars with windows on all sides providing plenty of daylight. So we could, in what many consider to be an ideal situation, start from scratch. But I rather prefer impossible and improbable sites and situations than these large open spaces. They force you to be more creative. Luckily, the completion by the property-developer took roughly two years, which gave us plenty of time to develop the plans in great detail. The loft consisted of two parts that were joined by an inner terrace that was transformed into a connecting space. The habitants use one part, the visitors the other. When necessary the two parts can be split into autonomous living units with the help of one simple partition wall, each with its own entrance. I also cut the space lengthwise by situating the day-zone up front and the night-zone at the back, behind a series of freestanding walls that created a box, giving the impression of floating freely in space. All walls are white or covered with afrormosia veneer, while furniture pieces such as the large office desk are in massive afrormosia, my favourite kind of wood, because of its rich grain. The epoxy floor was executed in two colours that were mixed on the spot – to obtain a more lively and durable result. And luckily there was also a handicap. The basic assumption was that the kitchen would stand central. So we decided that it should be the first thing people are confronted with when they enter. Since there was a difference in level between the living room and the entrance hall, we decided to bridge it by a catwalk that descends towards the kitchen and widens up at the table, forming an extension of the kitchen bench. Quite a spectacle when the guests enter!"

TIMBERLAND BENELUX, head office and flagship store, 2003, Aartselaar, Belgium –
"I was born on a sheep station in the arid Grampians area of Victoria, in south-west Australia, also known as the Great Outdoors.
So when the Benelux department of one of the outdoor lifestyle brands by excellence, Timberland, asked me to do the interior
of their new headquarters, it came as a particular challenge. All the more because it had to be installed in an environment that
was anything but outback, an industrial building in an industrial zone. The Flagship store included a wholesale showroom, offices
and a concept shop. I opted for a bridge and a two-storey tower, the kind of constructions that you usually find outdoors, by
using materials and building them in such a way that people would start to doubt if they were inside or out. On the other hand,
I sought to marry the concepts of a natural and industrial jungle, by combining wood with iron and steel, warm versus cold."

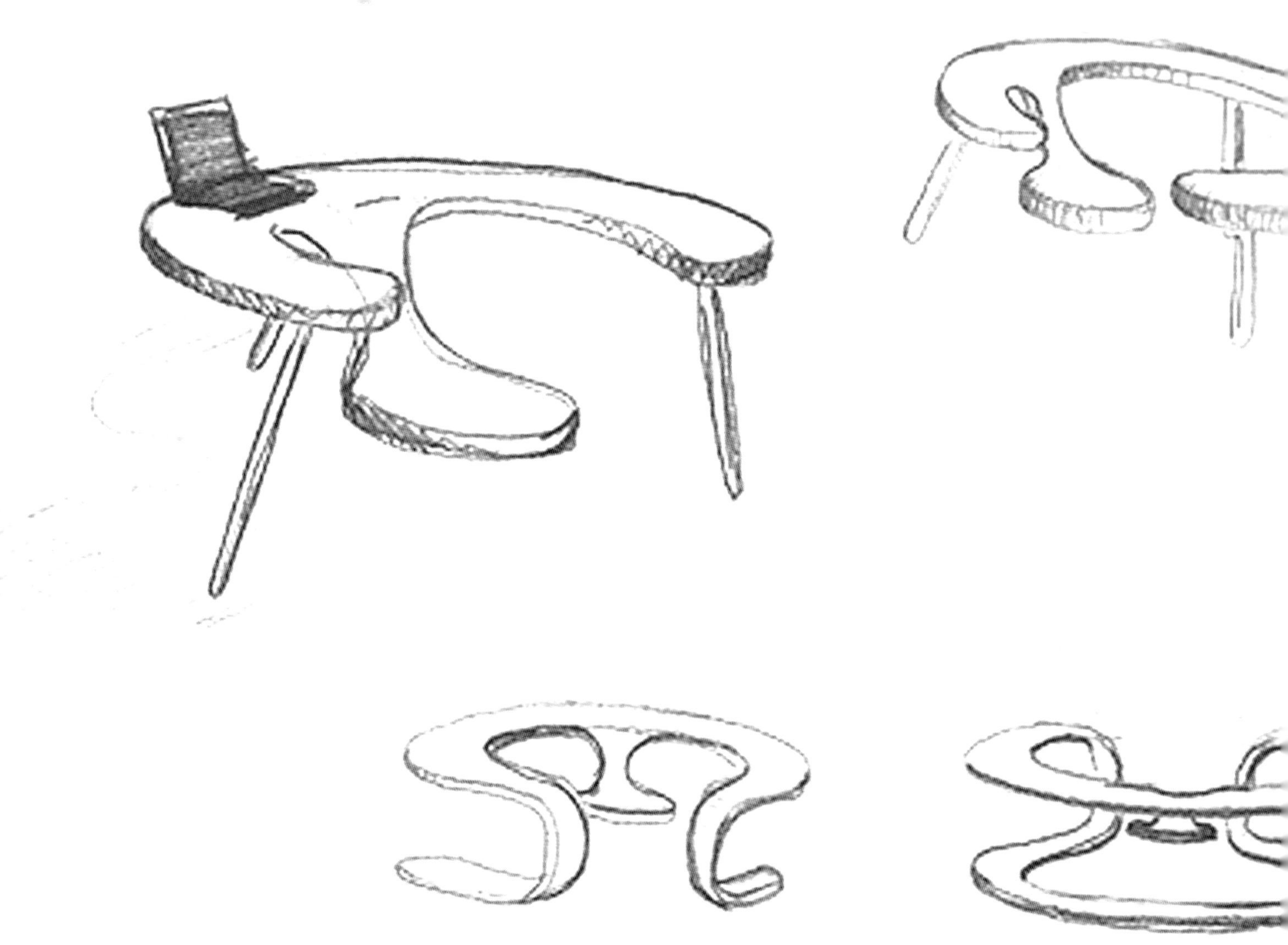

EASY RIDER, 2002 – "The most innovative Belgian manufacturer of office furniture, Bulo, asked me to design the newest addition to its *Carte Blanche* collection, a range that includes designs of some of the world's most renowned designers from the realms of architecture, fashion and interior design, such as Jean Nouvel, Ann Demeulemeester, Maarten Van Severen and Dirk Bikkembergs. Bulo had seen my *Man-Chi*, a massage chair on which you sit backwards. Their briefing was to design a relax-office. I aimed for something that would not only require minimal means to attain maximal flexibility in terms of versatility and mobility, but would also be humorous, playful and elegant. The result is a mobile object in which the seat of the *Man-Chi* remains essentially the same, but the back organically spreads into circular arms that embrace the user and can be used as a backrest, armrest or working surface. A desk and seat combined into one, to sit with a laptop and mobile phone near at hand, but also offering the warmth of a comfortable armchair. Viewed from above, the *Easy Rider* is no more than a simple circle, with a sunken part that serves as a seat and three legs with either casters or gliders. It's true that it resembles a *Baby Walker*, because of the suspended seat. We were originally even thinking of calling it by that name, but changed our minds because it might make people feel a little infantile. Still, it indicates the fun factor: Timberland Benelux asked me to design a new boardroom and I recommended them the *Easy Rider*. Immediately, the meetings seemed to take a totally different course. There's no head of the table, and much less hierarchy, since there is no table anymore, while all participants can move away or come closer as they please, be it only to show their approval or discontent – the interaction is phenomenal. Things become much more informal, and from the very onset the ice is broken with newcomers. Technically, there are several novelties. The wheels are like those of inline skates, while the frame is covered with three-dimensional upholstery. Instead of twelve pieces required to upholster the chair it only needs three. Since its introduction as the official chair of the Interieur Biennale 02, it has also become one of my most awarded designs. It won a *Red Dot Award*, an *Adex Platinum Award*, a *Henry van de Velde* prize and a *Good Design Award*. But what pleased me most was that it was the first piece in the *Carte Blanche* collection that was also commercially a hit."

A tale of
two worlds

Danny Venlet was born in 1958, from Dutch parents who had moved to Australia. His father Cornelis Nicolas Venlet, a specialist in biodynamic farming, had taken over a sheep station in outback Victoria three years earlier. However, rural life in the semi arid Grampians area was tough and after years of drought the family moved on. While on holiday in Europe, his father was offered a job. He accepted, and never returned to down under again. It was 1966. Danny and his older brother Nick went to a boarding school in the Netherlands. His younger brother Richard and his sister Ann settled with their parents in Germany. Three years later the family was reunited in Brussels, only to be split up again, due to the parents' divorce.

From Australia to Brussels...

Danny would later credit his early interest into art to his mother, who ran a doll studio, and his interest in ecology to his father. He was also taken up by architecture quite early: "Geometrical drawing was my thing at school, while I constantly kept refurbishing my room at home, creating bookshelves out of fibre cement tubes. It also means that my passion for the circular form was already present, but I had no idea one could make a living out of it. So when I had to decide on a profession, I ended up studying medicine. Partly on my father's advice, but also because of the same passion and fascination that would later make me decide to become an interior architect and designer. I wanted to study people, their habits, rituals and motives. I wanted to influence their interaction with the environment. It didn't take long before I realised that studying medicine was above all about chemistry, physics and pills. Man himself didn't really seem all that important. So I stopped."

Venlet went on studying applied computer sciences at the University of Brussels, but left halfway through the year, to go and live on a Kibbutz in Israel. It was there that he decided, after three months of hard labour, that he might 'do something with interior'. Back in Brussels he went to study interior architecture at the same school where his brother Richard studied art, the St Lukas Institute for Architecture and Visual Arts, where he is a lecturer now. He wasn't exactly a model student. After a difficult start, in which he had to catch up with basics like sketching, he became part of a group committed to reforming the whole design education system. Nevertheless he graduated cum laude in 1984, with a dissertation called Natuur en de Muur (Nature and the Wall), focusing on a proposal for vertical gardens, panels of grass that could be fixed on the wall: "I had worked in gardens to pay my studies, and ecology still ruled my thoughts."

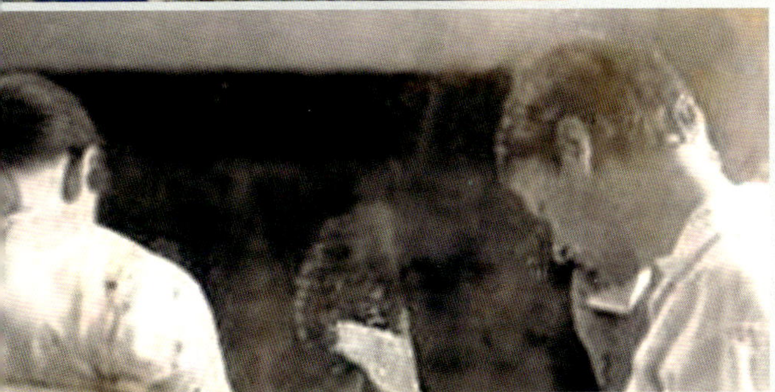

It was also this passion for nature that made Venlet decide to return to Australia and the Great Outdoors: "I was a nomad by birth, just like my parents. I had visited more than ten schools as a boy. I wanted to broaden my horizons and still had this Australian passport. So I decided to go and live in Sydney for six months." He ended up staying there for twelve years, before he came back and settled in Brussels.

A lack of means first brought him to an aunt in Brisbane, Queensland, where he found a job as a model-maker at the Peter Sands studio. But deciding that Sydney was the city to be, he soon moved on, to become a model-maker at Rice Daubney architects first, and to work as an interior designer for Inarch and finally with what is now called Burley Katon Halliday (BKH).

Venlet worked with BKH for two and a half years, mainly on the Powerhouse museum in Sydney. The museum, situated in a turn-of-the-century industrial building that formerly provided the electricity for the local tram network, opened its doors in 1988. Venlet had been partly responsible for creating a setting for the design and decoration collection with curator Christopher Thompson, a highly detailed job, which extended to designing a place for every object. It became a crucial experience: "It was mainly there that I learned to look at furniture, jewels and other objects, and what makes them work."

Following a cooperation with Neil Burley, also in 1988, Venlet founded Daffodil design with Marc Newson and Tina Engelen one year later: "When I met Marc, I had just started my first furniture pieces. Marc was a jewellery designer by education, but had been asked to turn a seedy Laundromat into the Andoni fashion store in Paddington. He felt kind of uncertain and called for my help. That's how the partnership started."

Andoni's challenging simplicity was later described as its main virtue. Glimpsed from the street through the huge glass face, the impression was teasingly spare. On the right wall aluminium portholes showed off brightly lit trinkets, whereas on the left wall a long rail of designer clothing reached back toward the changing rooms. Bisecting the space with a row of floor lights, like a runway, beckoned the visitors inside.

The clarity and light-hearted feeling for Pop that emanated from the project, became the hallmark of Daffodil's approach, and spearheaded a successful chain of notable jobs, including three furniture showrooms for DéDéCé in Melbourne, Brisbane and Auckland, New Zealand. However Newson was soon highly engrossed in his own career, in Tokyo and elsewhere; when Daffodil accepted its biggest and most memorable project, the Burdekin

Hotel refurbishment, the collaboration had already virtually come to an end. Venlet ventured on to start his own studio, VIA, or Venlet Interior Architecture in 1991, and established himself as an independent designer.

… to Brussels again.

By the time he returned to Belgium, five years later, his portfolio comprised many prestigious projects, next to the ones previously mentioned: the *Ke-Zu* furniture showrooms, the *Parmalat* coffee shop in Darlinhurst, the *Q* chain of nightclubs, *Kinsella's bar* and a series of residential projects. In view of some of these refurbishments he had designed a number of notable pieces of furniture, such as the *Q stool* and the *Burdekin* stool and table. But although this had drawn the attention of the international press, who credited him as the designer who had revolutionized nightlife, his success remained limited: "I had been a regular exhibitor at the Salone del Mobile in Milan and elsewhere in Europe, where considerable interest was shown. But once I returned to Australia, it was a matter of out of sight, out of mind. Australia may be a huge continent but the market was limited. Companies mainly produced for the local market and imported furniture was expensive. It had given me the opportunity to create my own furniture for a similar price. But finally I decided to go and work in Europe, albeit not on a permanent basis."

Private circumstances were to decide differently. After Venlet had moved with his then wife, the artist Piki Verschueren, and his two daughters, Mona and Astrid, to Belgium in 1996, he was to stay there. Coming back had seemed timely because it coincided with a newfound energy and interest in Belgian design, fashion and art. "But I soon experienced that people don't receive you with open arms after you've been away for twelve years, despite your portfolio. It took me at least five years before I succeeded in working up to the level I had reached when leaving Australia."

Today, Venlet's studio is still based in the centre of Brussels, in a 19th century house and former button factory, where he lives with his new wife, the designer Evi Lippens, and his three daughters.

Award-winning objects such as the *Easy Rider*, a mobile workstation he developed for Bulo, the *D2V2* light for Dark and, more recently, the *Shower* and *Lylo* waterbed he created for Viteo, enhanced his international renown in the world of design. Most of his work however is still situated in the field of interior architecture: his projects range from private mansions, over showrooms and shops, The *Lexington* bar and *Music Room* nightclub in the former GPO building in Melbourne, to a relaxation centre in Antwerp, libraries, temporary exhibitions for the International Red Cross and offices for large companies such as Timberland.

Max Borka

FLYSCREEN, 1992 – "From the very beginning, my objects have been the result of an interaction between art and function. The functional was and is the starting point, and steers the process in every detail. But I also tend to give my designs a sculptural quality so that they can stand on their own when they are not in use. This early concern with the sculptural is probably best demonstrated by the *FlyScreen* and a series of other one-offs that – contrary to almost all my other early designs – were not created in function of a very specific architectural project, but were specially made for an exhibition at the Yuill Crowley Gallery in Sydney. The collection was the result of experiments that were simultaneously exercises in the illusory and economical use, and tried to create three-dimensional objects from two-dimensional surfaces by opposing concave forms. The knowledge that these objects were only one-offs, and never would have to comply with production criteria, gave me much more freedom. The *FlyScreen*, which also serves as a space-divider, consists of fabric that has been stretched over a wooden frame, with its pattern heightening the optical illusion – as if the whole object is imploding, an effect that would often return in my work later on."

POWDERHORSE STOOL, POWDERHORSE CHAISE LONGUE, GOLD, VAULT TABLE, BEHIND REST, 1991-1995 – "Together with *FlyScreen* and *Gestalt*, these one-offs were specially created for an exhibition at the Yuill Crowley Gallery in Sydney. They formed part of my research into a series of polarities that would also stand central to most of my subsequent work, such as the two- and three-dimensional, convex and concave forms, art and design, the sculptural and functional or the real and the illusory. They are all based on the same principle: the deceptively heavy but in fact extremely lightweight furniture pieces consist of nothing more than a welded and polished aluminium sheet of only 3 mm thick, or an equivalent in MDF, or varnished bent poplar triplex. While looking massive from the outside, they are totally empty on the inside. Again, it is a matter of minimal means and maximal effect. The user is almost sitting on air, while the skin of these objects coincides origami-like with their structure, and obtains its strength from the interplay of curves. The circle is the basic form, even when this is not always visible. The outline of the objects is defined by negative forms, the kind of silhouettes you keep when you a cut a circle out of a piece of paper. I opted for these negative forms because the objects had to be receptive – the human body representing the positive half. There are some variations between these objects. With the *Gold* chair, the illusion of a heavy volume is stressed by a large conic piercing, while the sheet is treated with a gold and translucent powder coating with a crackle effect. *The Vault Table* is decorated with marqueterie – in a similar effort to provide the skin with a feeling of massiveness. Finally, the *Behind Rest* differs from the other objects because it can be used in two different positions, serving as a chair or pouf, and because it is made from glued MDF-discs with aluminium ends."

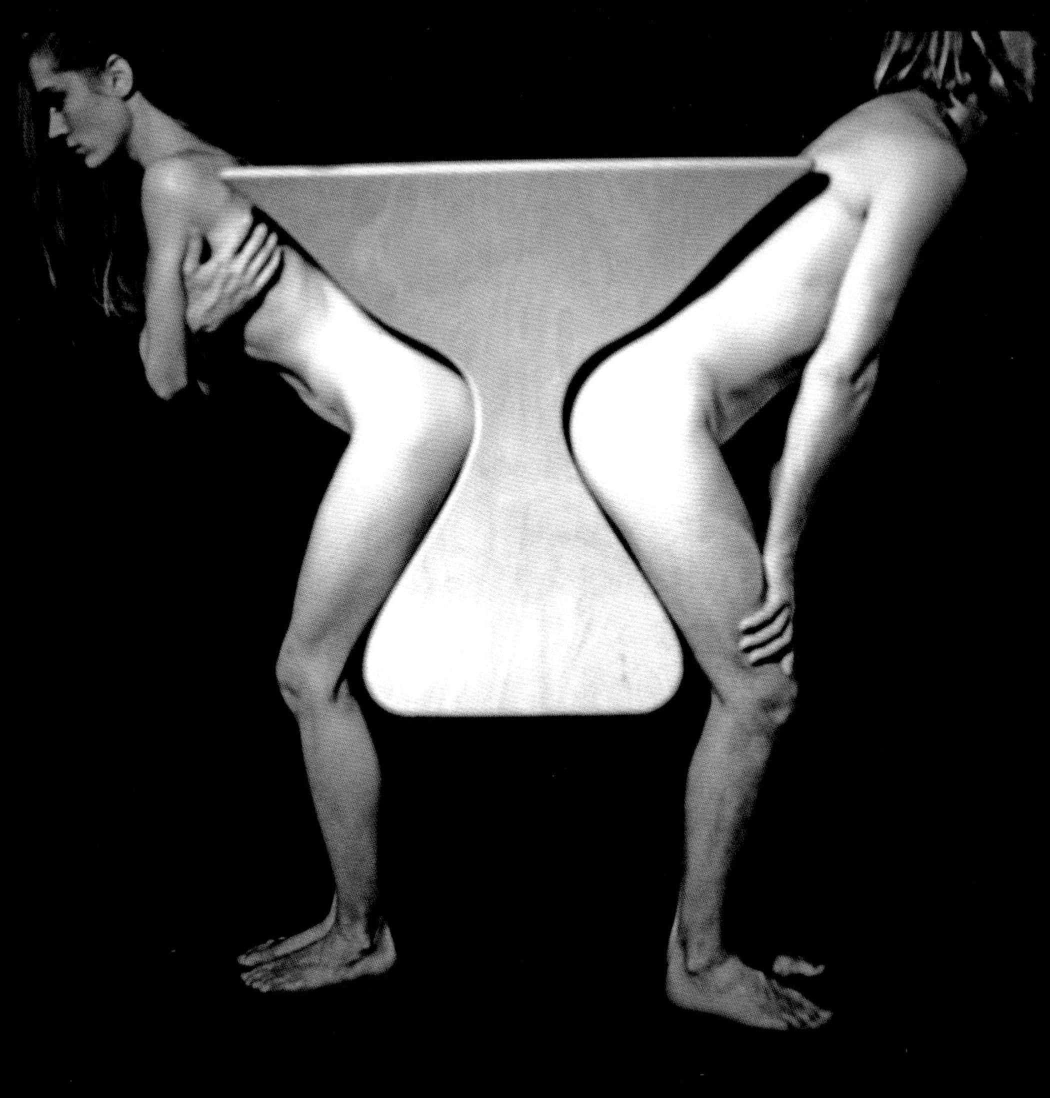

GESTALT, 1992 – "An ergonomic Australian bus seat provided the inspiration for this piece, that was also created for the exhibition at Yuill Crowley Gallery. It took the interaction between the negative curves of the furniture pieces and the positive curves of the user to the extreme, without limiting myself to circular forms, as had been the case with the *Powderhorse* stool and *Chaise Longue* and the *Gold*. My own body and that of a friend provided the curves. Design has always been to me first and foremost a matter of psychology. The name of this piece refers to similar experiments and tools in *Gestalt* therapy, such as the *Rubin Vase*, the famous illustrations in which the viewer can recognize different images in the same silhouette, according to the position taken: a vase, or the profiles of two faces. What you see in it also gives something away about your state of mind. The same dilemma is to be found in this hybrid piece of furniture: a simple rotation turns the chair into a table, when upright. The original mould was destroyed in a fire, so that the number of copies remains limited to three – two in curved plywood, the other in fibreglass, now part of the collection of the *Powerhouse Museum* in Sydney, Australia."

DESIGN AS DESIGN, exhibition, 1997 – "Immediately after my return to Belgium, after a 12-year career in Australia, I was asked to co-curate an exhibition on Belgian design. The selection of the artists was not programmatic. There was no shared manifesto, no common ground other than the fact that they all lived in Belgium. Some were already internationally famous, such as Ann Demeulemeester and Maarten Van Severen. Others – Myriam Burnaz, Tony Hendrickx and Traces De Doigts – were quite unknown. I mainly showed the collection I had developed for the Yuill Crowley Gallery in Sydney, and added one architectural element: a huge stocking in transparent textile that diagonally traversed this wonderful space and somehow tried to bind everything together. Its form was defined by the fact that it started as a rectangle upstairs and ended in an ellipse downstairs, while showing all the intermediary stages. The upper end was also attached to an open window on the first floor. Looking through that opening people could discover a Q stool at the other end."

PARMALAT, coffee shop, 1993, Darlinghurst, Sydney, Australia –

"I love to work in spaces that suffer from a handicap. They leave you with no other choice than to be extremely inventive and also force you to come up with very site-specific solutions, turning the disadvantage into an advantage, the handicap into a trump. There's nothing more frustrating than the ideal space, such as a beautifully empty loft. As soon as you bring something into that space, that loft feeling is gone. I also love solutions that have the simplicity and obviousness of the Egg of Columbus. The specific problem of the site that had to be transformed into the *Parmalat* coffee shop, later renamed *Latteria*, was that the available space was 10 m deep by 4 m high, behind a high glass façade that spanned the street and could entirely be opened like a harmonica. However, it was also extremely narrow – barely 2,5 m. In these circumstances it didn't really seem appropriate to install the kitchen and counter at the back. So we attached the kitchen facilities onto one of the long sidewalls and installed the tables and chairs along the other, while eliminating the traditional counter in between. The obligation to create such a barrier, imposed by health code, was avoided by drawing a borderline on the ground. A more open and informal relationship between the customers and the personnel has always been my primal concern when designing bars and restaurants, and our move in *Parmalat* proved to be extremely effective. Doing away with the counter as a barrier created a much more homely atmosphere. The solution we came up with created the uniqueness of the place, making it trendsetting, while providing an enormous publicity. Its success can also be measured from the fact that it is still there after all these years. For this project I also created barrel-like wooden stools with a bowling-ball thumb hole for portability, to be easily taken outside, as an alternative to the ubiquitous milk crates used by all other cafés in the area to accommodate the extra sidewalk trade. Its wood contrasts nicely to the functional surfaces of the interior: the stainless steel of the kitchen, the spackle finished wall that survived the renovations, the tiled floor and steps that lead to an elevated seating area at the back where customers enjoy a spectacular open view to the front."

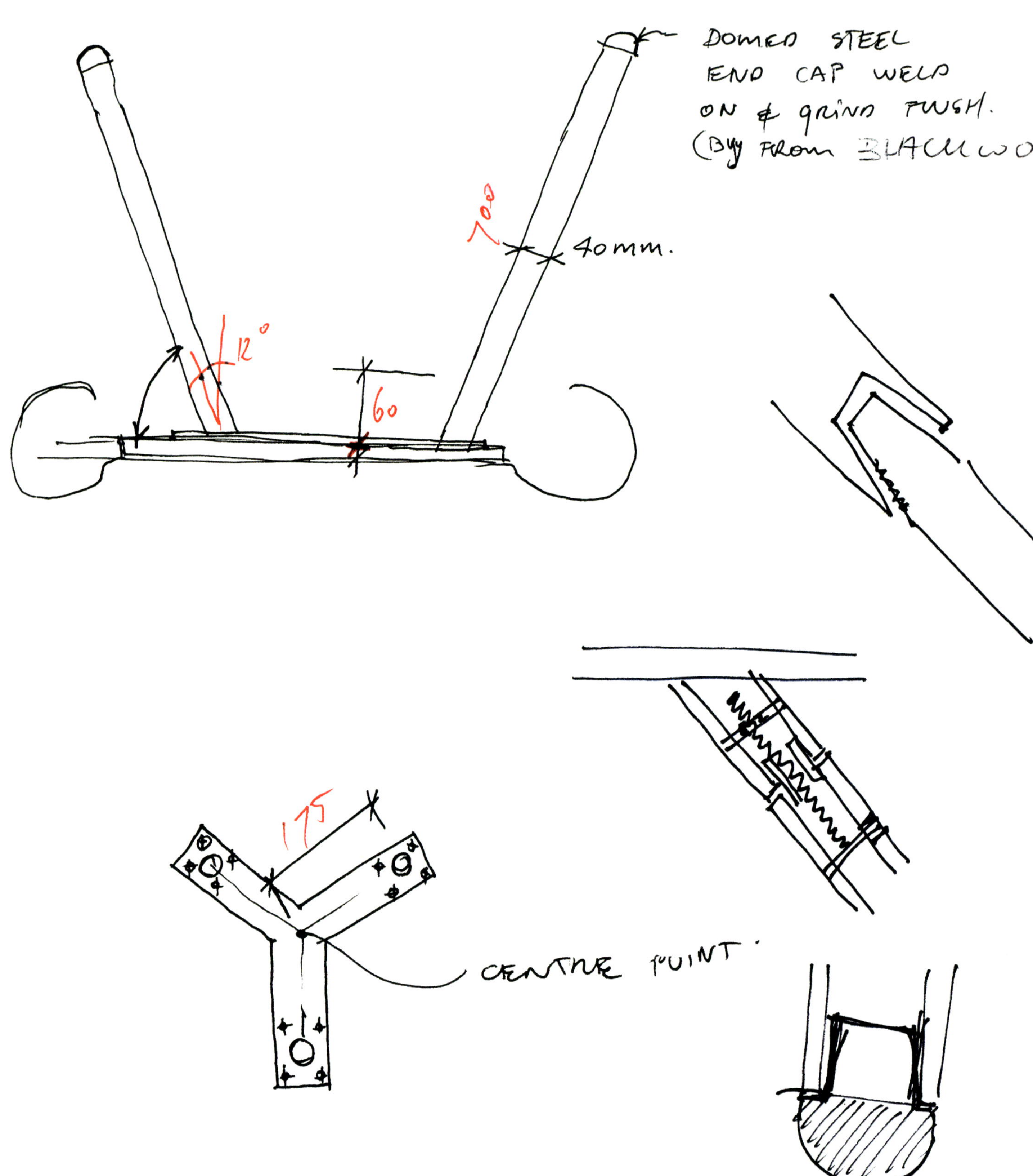

BURDEKIN TABLE, 1990 – "My early efforts to create an economical three-dimensional volume through the manipulation of a two-dimensional surface had its first commercial application in this table, which was originally designed for the bar of the *Burdekin Hotel* in Sydney. The round and broadly rimmed tabletop is turned out of a single anodised aluminium sheet of only 3 mm thick, and is supported by three cylindrical legs in stainless steel that are screwed into the underside of the tabletop. The tabletop is available in gold, silver, electric blue and yellow."

BURDEKIN BAR, 1990, Darlinghurst, Sydney, Australia – "*The Burdekin Hotel* was not really a hotel. It only carried that name in order to obtain a licence for a restaurant and bar. It was housed in a historical landmark building that dated from 1840. It is a strange building, with a triangular floor plan resembling a piece of cake. It is positioned at the gateway to Sydney's Oxford Street, a top location in the city centre, near Hyde Park, but it had somehow never succeeded in fully exploiting that strategic position. It seemed to turn its back to the street. On a young continent like Australia a heritage building of that age is considered extremely old and rare. And yet, at least when I started as an interior architect, Australians were neither familiar nor really interested in the idea of preserving this kind of monuments. Speculators wanted to tear the building down and replace it with an apartment block, but luckily other investors succeeded in buying the building and saved it. The 'function rooms' were refurbished in several phases: a public bar on the ground floor, a bar in the cellar, and a dining room that moved from the third to the first floor. The budget was generous, and I was given carte blanche – something Australian project developers are extremely good in. Two adjoining bars had to be merged, which meant that partition walls had to be demolished – but apart from that I tried to treat the building's history with the greatest respect. While others had always tried to make the remarkable but difficult triangular outline rectangular, I restored it as much as possible, together with the existing heritage features and decorations that dated from the building's origin, or had been added later on, such as the art deco windows and the fibrous plaster art nouveau ceiling, possibly dating from 1912, that was revealed during the removal of a false ceiling installed during the 1938 renovation. It partly explains why I decided to combine my *Burdekin* tables that were already in production, with old *Thonet* chairs. Next to the new tables, counter, and stools – new chairs would have been too much. I needed a neutralising element and the *Thonet* chairs lent themselves perfect to the situation. The complex pattern of the ceiling was framed by a grid of beams that reflected the layout of the floor space. We kept an open plan, and created a framework for the historical elements that had been preserved. This frame mainly consisted of some custom designed elements that served as 'contact points' and were radically contemporary in materials, look, and style, with curvy minimalist forms that seemed to radiate from the existing columns and the equally radiating design of the parquetry floor. The main element was the elliptical bar counter, built from two identically moulded but mirroring fibreglass sections, bolted together under a laminated wooden top. It was quite spectacular because it didn't have the traditional groove in which Australians throw their cigarette butts at the bottom, but seamlessly went over in the floor where the curvy pattern continued in the pattern of wooden blocks. From the public side its concave wall was counter-posed by maroon leather-covered stools that were also specially designed for this project and had the shape of a punching ball, adding a sense of humour to an otherwise restrained approach. The overall effect was described in the media as 'Space lounge meets Vienna coffee house'. Likewise the floor was a combination of wood and epoxy, old and new, an experiment that had been a shot in the dark, but had a great result, while the clean feeling of the space was reinforced by restricting colour to a subtle mixture of creams and browns. The counter was clad in a smoky, weathered look, while the stools were clad in old saddle-leather. The walls were plastered with Stucco Lustro, a mixture of plaster and marble dust. The overall look was that of an old weathered bar, which was exactly what I wanted, because I wanted to make the place as accessible as possible. That's why I also installed a new door to the street, and moved the restaurant from the third to the first floor. The scheme has been published widely and was hailed as 'creating a new tradition in Australian bars', 'Redefining the pub', while the local Art Deco Society was so impressed that it added the bar to its Sunday walk which before only consisted of houses and bridges."

BURDEKIN BARSTOOL, 1990 – "Australia may be a big country, its market is quite small. There were hardly any producers to be found when I started as a designer and the few that were, weren't interested in what happened elsewhere. They only produced for the local market. This not only explains why I decided to move to Europe but also why I started to design my own furniture, When I was asked to design the bar and restaurant of the *Burdekin Hotel* for example, I simply could not find what I wanted. So I ended up designing a barstool that was meant to be complementary to the concave and hollowed out front of the bar. I like my objects to have a clear outline. So I gave the ball that serves as a seat a seamless lining that stretches out downward organically into a tear that touches the round base on the floor in one single spot, while hiding all the technicalities that might be considered disturbing. It turned the barstool into something surreal: as if the ball was floating extremely lightweight in a bag that is held upside down. Time and again the stool has been compared to a punching ball. That is ok to me, but it was never my intention to evoke that association. I simply wanted to create 'a third leg' for the user. It is made from an upright steel post that supports the injection-moulded and upholstered foam. There have been many different editions such as the *Burdekin Freestanding*, a lower version with four foot-pegs forming a cross in chrome-plated steel. My favourite is the one that was upholstered in a batik canvas and decorated by my former wife, Piki Verschueren, using Giovanni Matteo Contavini's *Florentine World Map* of 1506, as part of the *Homage to Columbus* project by Wunderhaus in Munich."

BURDEKIN DINING ROOM, Darlinghurst, Australia / **BURDEKIN LIGHT** and **BURDEKIN BASIN**, 1991 –
"In the second stage of the renovation of the *Burdekin Hotel* the restaurant was moved from the third to the first floor. A corridor split the restaurant in two. The smaller, triangular room offered a view of Sydney's skyline and harbour; the other rectangular room had an outlook on Oxford Street, where the Burdekin is located. Again, we tried to preserve as much as possible the valuable original elements of the building, such as the art deco windows and the former transformations dating back to the beginning of the 20th century and 1938. We mainly focused on the dead corners of the difficult triangular space by adding some beech-veneered waiter-stations. The material and interplay of curves and counter curves of these stations were intended as a playful reference to the art deco style, taking its language to the extreme by way of counterpoise, and creating a kind of imploding furniture. Instead of doing away with the already existing fireplace, we decided to highlight it by integrating it into one of the stations that magnified its form and made it resemble a giant mouth. The walls were punctuated with the *Burdekin Lights* that I had specially designed for this project, made out of curved glass on a chrome plated support. The glass has been burned and tinted in yellow with a silver emulsion – very art deco, just like the basins that were specially designed for the public bathroom. I've always been striving for a new kind of functionalism. From a strictly utilitarian point not even the smallest detail is superfluous. And yet, the design – curvy and minimal – should also be sculptural and seduce when not in use. These modular basins, that were provided with a junction that is strictly speaking just a container for guest towels, are a good example."

BURDEKIN DINING ROOM
THE BURDEKIN

GPO LEXINGTON and **MUSIC ROOM**, bar and nightclub, 2005, Melbourne, Australia – "After its restoration in 2004, the historic and heritage-listed Melbourne General Post Office (GPO) had been reconverted into a fashion, food and shopping Mecca, the Bourke Street Mall. The entrepreneur, Ian Robertson, for whom I had created the Q bars, asked me to create two major entertainment venues: the *Lexington*, a mammoth bar and restaurant and *The Music Room*, a nightclub. They had to be totally in line with the elegance and sophistication of the place and its stunning Victorian style architecture – grand in scale and rich in style. So we highlighted the grand archways, 7 m high ceilings and huge period windows with enormous *Swarovski* crystal chandeliers that were specially created for the occasion. We draped the private enclaves and added some contemporary elements, such as a giant balloon and a line of my own *D2V2 lights*, hovering over a giant custom-designed counter, sculpted out of cottonwood and fibreglass. My main concern when designing bars has always been to introduce new forms of nightlife, based on a more intense and open relationship between customers and personnel. In the *Music Room*, installed in a huge attic, we lined up five small counters, luminous pods, each put on a pedestal, and each ran by a different barman. Customers have to choose their favourite one, which stimulates the competition between the barman and at the same time their bond with the clients. The result is also a powerful theatrical effect that is heightened by the giant air balloon in the middle of the room. As the night wears on, the whole area in front of the bars transforms into one big dance floor. Further features are the Black and White Room that are also painted as such, each situated in a tower at opposite ends. In the *Lexington* a giant bar bordering one side of the room, with integrated booth seating at both ends, gives the people the impression of sitting in the counter."

SWIRL, 2006, Decosit fair, Brussels, Belgium –
"As part of Decosit, a major trade fair for the textile industry, Matali Crasset, the Belgian designer Will Erens and myself, were asked to create an 'innovative box', exploring the relationship between textile and respectively water, light and sound. While focusing on the interplay between textile and light, I created a double spiral with a transparent pierced cloth, that lead the visitors to the centre of the box, and kept on changing in atmosphere – while reflecting and absorbing the light. *Swarowski* crystals were added between the two fabrics, starting with a few and ending in the middle in abundance".

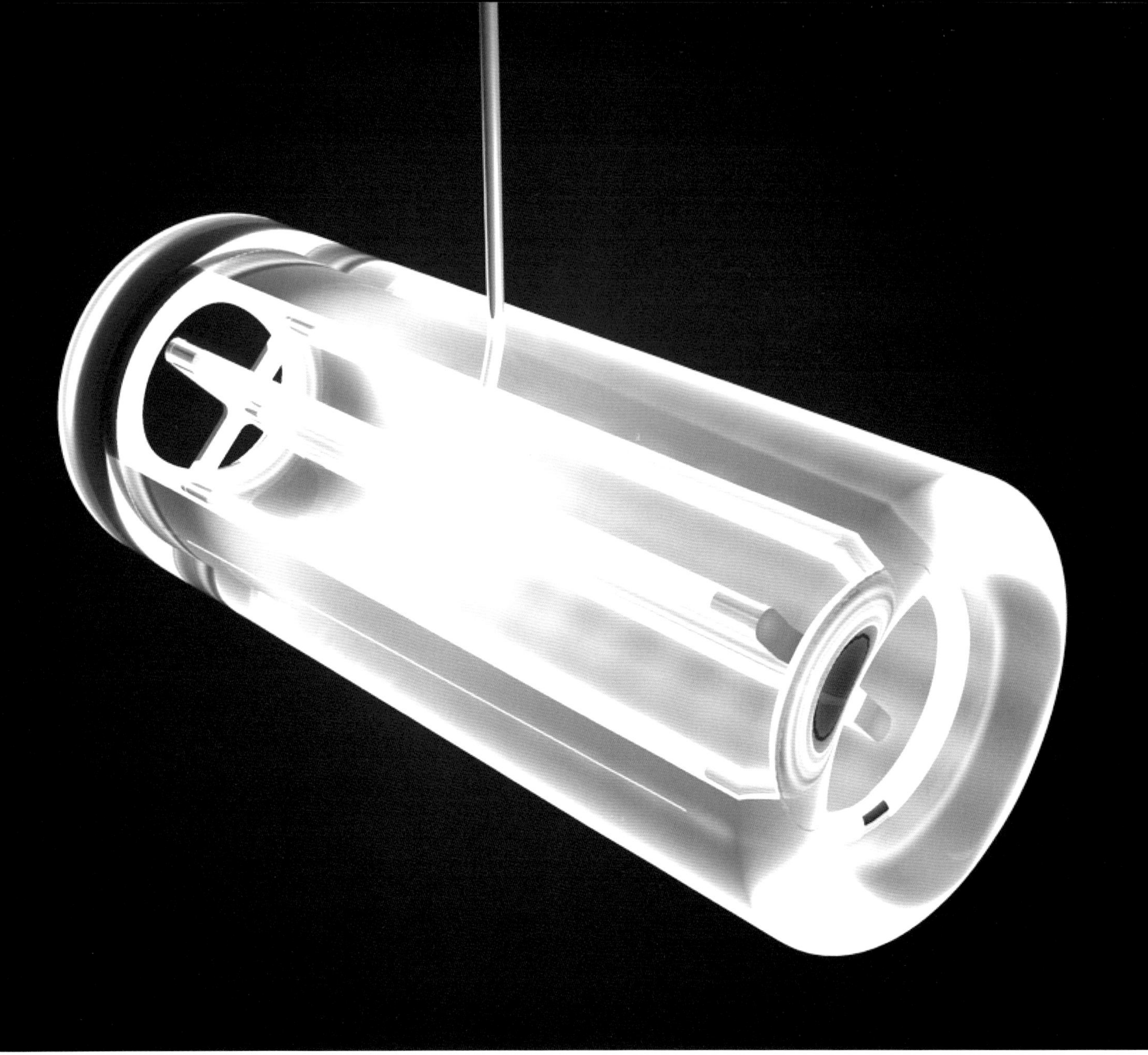

D2V2, 2004 – "It is probably not only every minimalist's but simply every designer's dream to design a light with a fitting that remains invisible, as if the artificial light were totally natural. Therefore, the *D2V2* may seem rather unnatural. It is gigantic. All this had to do with the briefing I received from the Belgian design company Dark, who specializes in this kind of eye-catching lights. They commissioned a light that would not only draw all the attention to itself, but would also serve as a creator of atmosphere, a striking piece of decoration. I created a light that I wanted reminiscent of a dotted line, but is repeatedly compared to the engine of an airplane. The floating effect grows with the number of lights that are hung together, creating the spectre of a fleet of bombers crossing the night sky, which is enhanced by the fact that the inner TL-lights don't seem to touch the cylinder in translucent polyethylene that forms the outer skin. It's probably one of the clearest examples of this strategy that I seem to have in common with Pop artists: to create objects that take their inspiration from the vernacular of popular imagination, such as punching balls, turbans, or baby walkers, and the visions and dreams these objects trigger in the subliminal, from heroic sports to Arabian Nights."

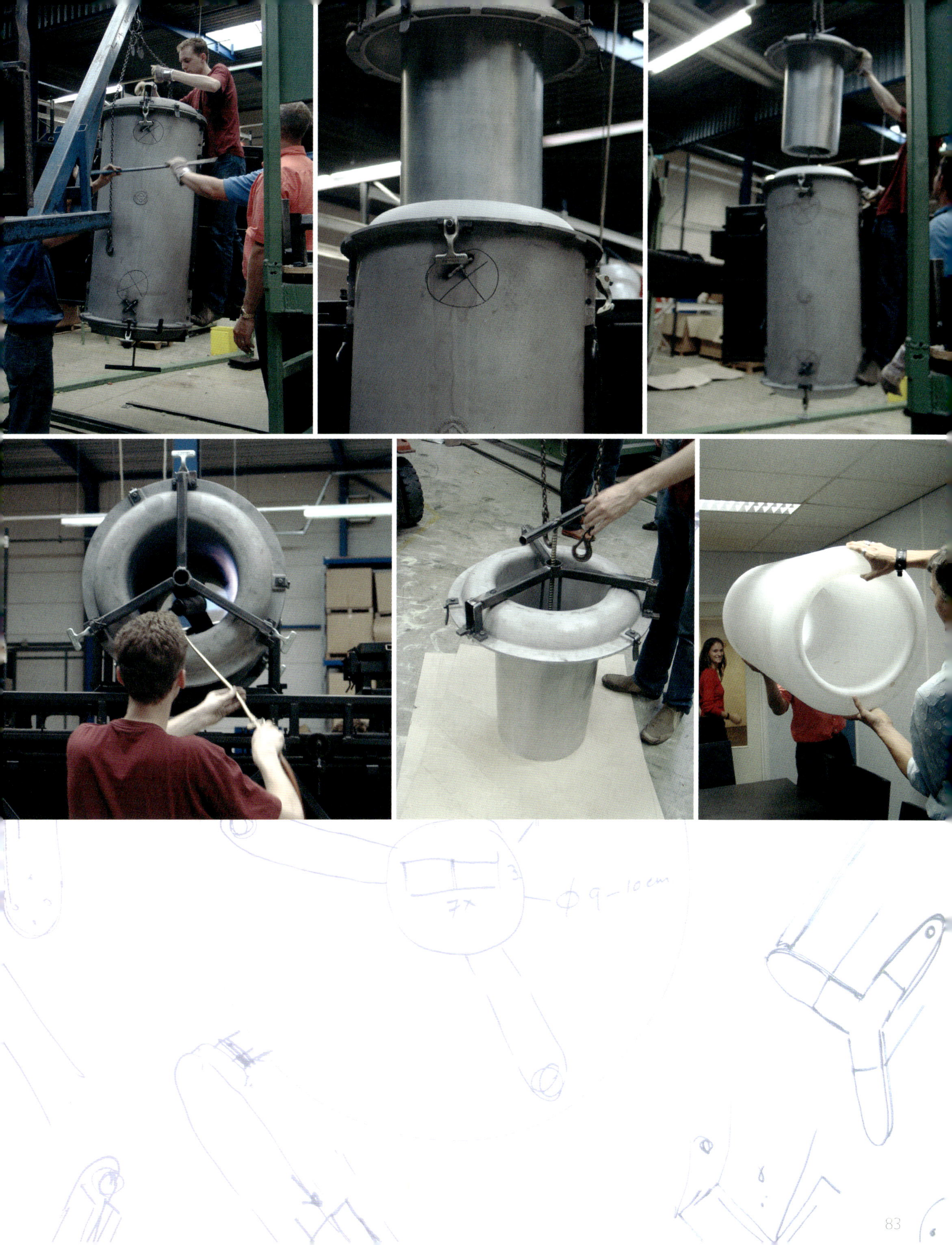

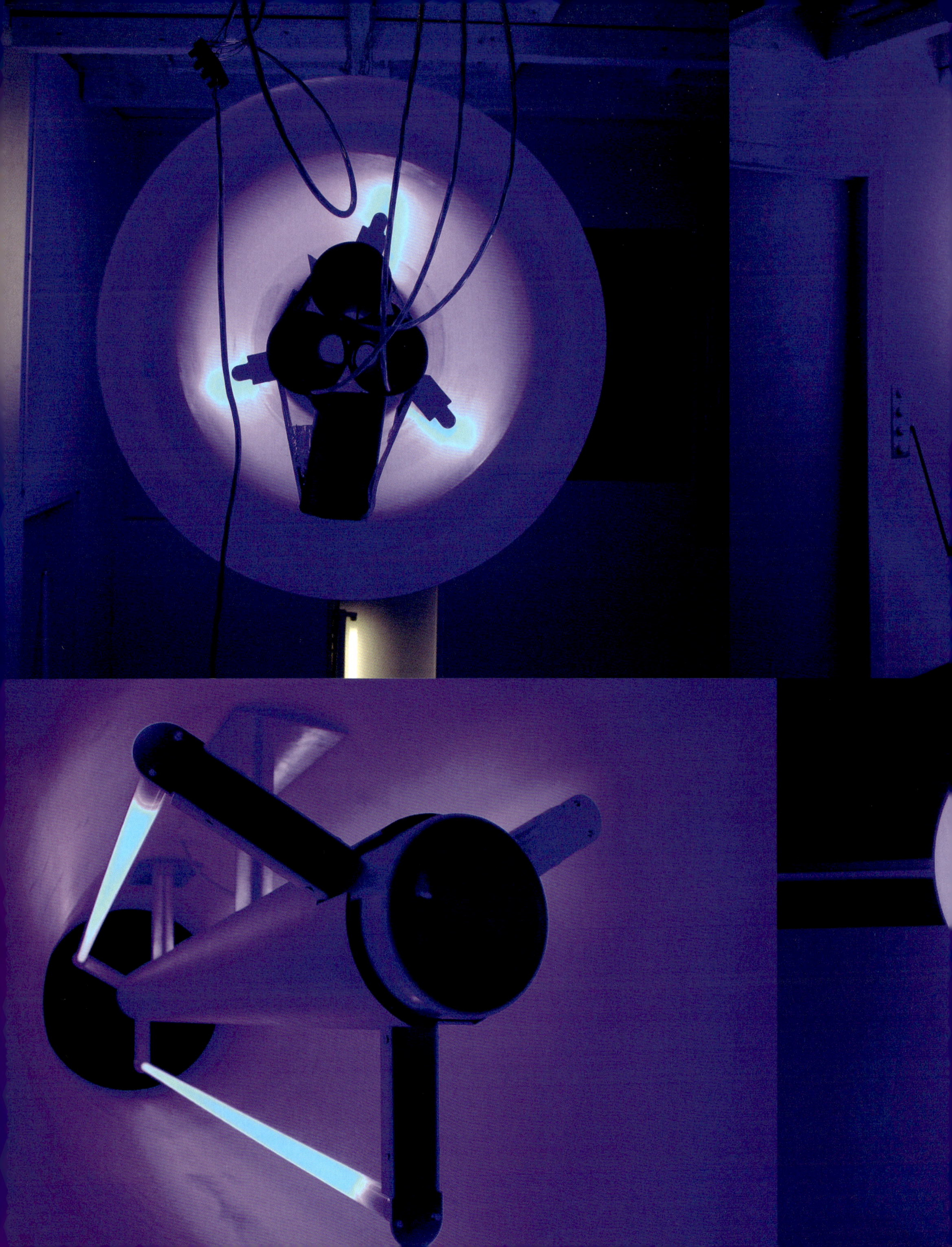

4
3
COMING SOON
www.SonyPictures.net
FÉVRIER 2006
FEBRUARI 2006

MINI CONCEPT CAR, fair stand, 2006, European Motor Show, Brussels – "When the Benelux department of Mini was informed by its headquarters that it would be impossible to show any of the new concept cars at the next edition of the European Motor Show in Brussels, it was decided that the three new concept cars would be shown anyway, but as a 3D-projection. The task was far from easy. We only disposed of a space measuring 9,72 by 13,5 m, and were limited in height. The box that would serve as *Mini-lounge* had to be totally isolated, as the sound could not exceed 80 db. Last but not least the stand-builder only had two weeks to construct the lounge. Visitors could register at the desk outside the black box for the Mini Design show that lasted 15 minutes and were handed 3D spectacles to watch the computer steered projection. There were 9 sessions a day, allowing no more then 30 people per session. The box was furnished with furniture designed by myself such as the *IceCube*, the *Q stools* and the *D2V2 lights*."

MINI CD BOX, 2007 – "The peculiar form of this CD-holder comes from the fact that it was the car brand Mini BMW that asked us to design such a box. The idea was to go for something minimal and sculptural, while avoiding a design that would be superfluous as a product. The wish of my client was to have a promotional tool that would be striking and seducing and comply with the image of Mini. And of course, the box had to be strong and protective. I came up with two flat plastic shells with a curvy rim that were screwed together by a hidden device in the middle, and unscrewed to reveal the CD. A hole in the rim not only brings a parking disc to mind, but also allows the names of the songs and musicians to be read when the disc is turned."

MOTOROLA, 2001 – "As part of an installation that was shown in *Things to Come*, an exhibition on the future of design, and one of the highlights of *Transit*, a design route through Brussels, Motorola asked me and some other Brussels designers to create a personalised version of their new cell phone, the V66. I incorporated a picture on its flap and covered it with warmth sensitive paint. When rubbing the paint with the thumb, the picture reveals itself, but it disappears again once the caressing stops. The cell phone thus turned into a kind of amulet, while the rubbing had something quite erotic."

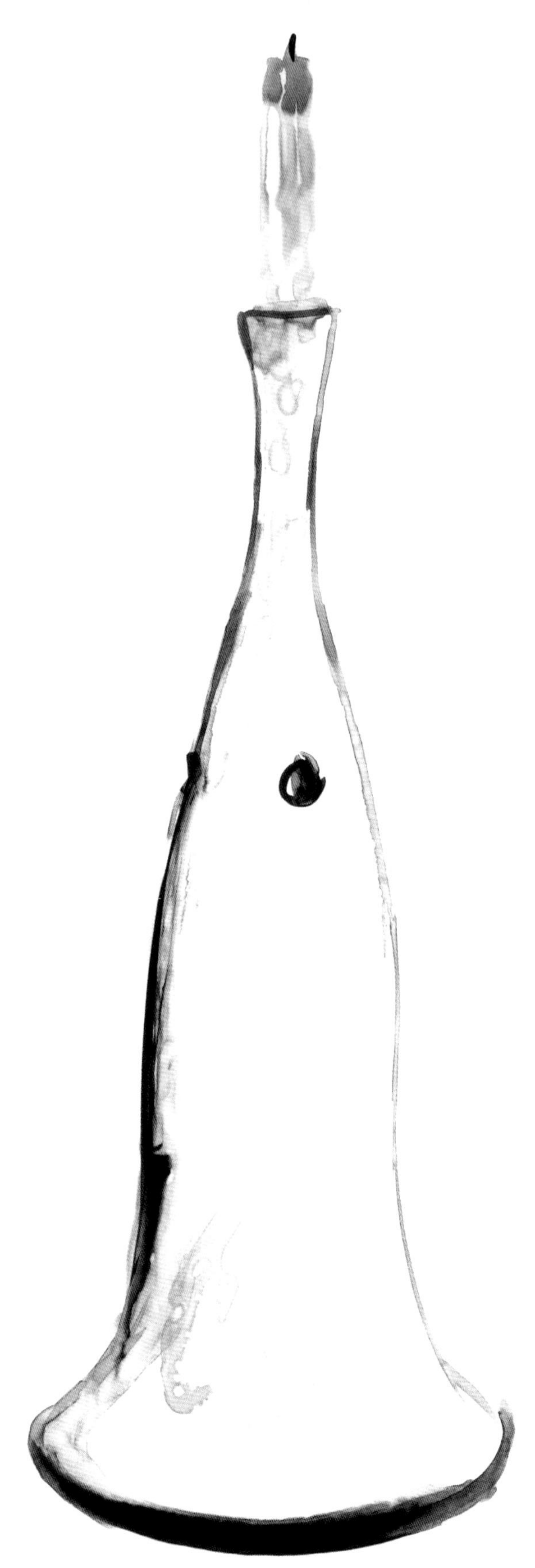

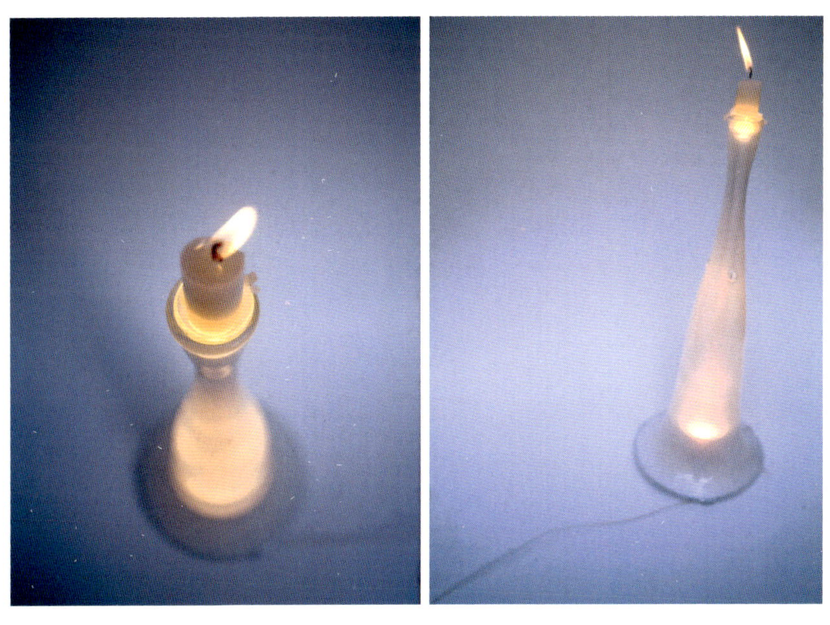

CANDLELIGHT, 1993 – "Not only two different light sources were combined in this lamp, but also two different worlds and periods, old and new, traditional and contemporary, natural and industrial, romantic and rational. I always wondered why this never happened before. The top of this restyled laboratory bottle in sandblasted glass can hold a candle while the inside of the bottle can be lit up with a dimmable low voltage electric lighting. The two kinds of soft lighting do not compete but complement each other. The whole also has a ghostly appearance, which I tried to enhance with the form and opaqueness of the bottle."

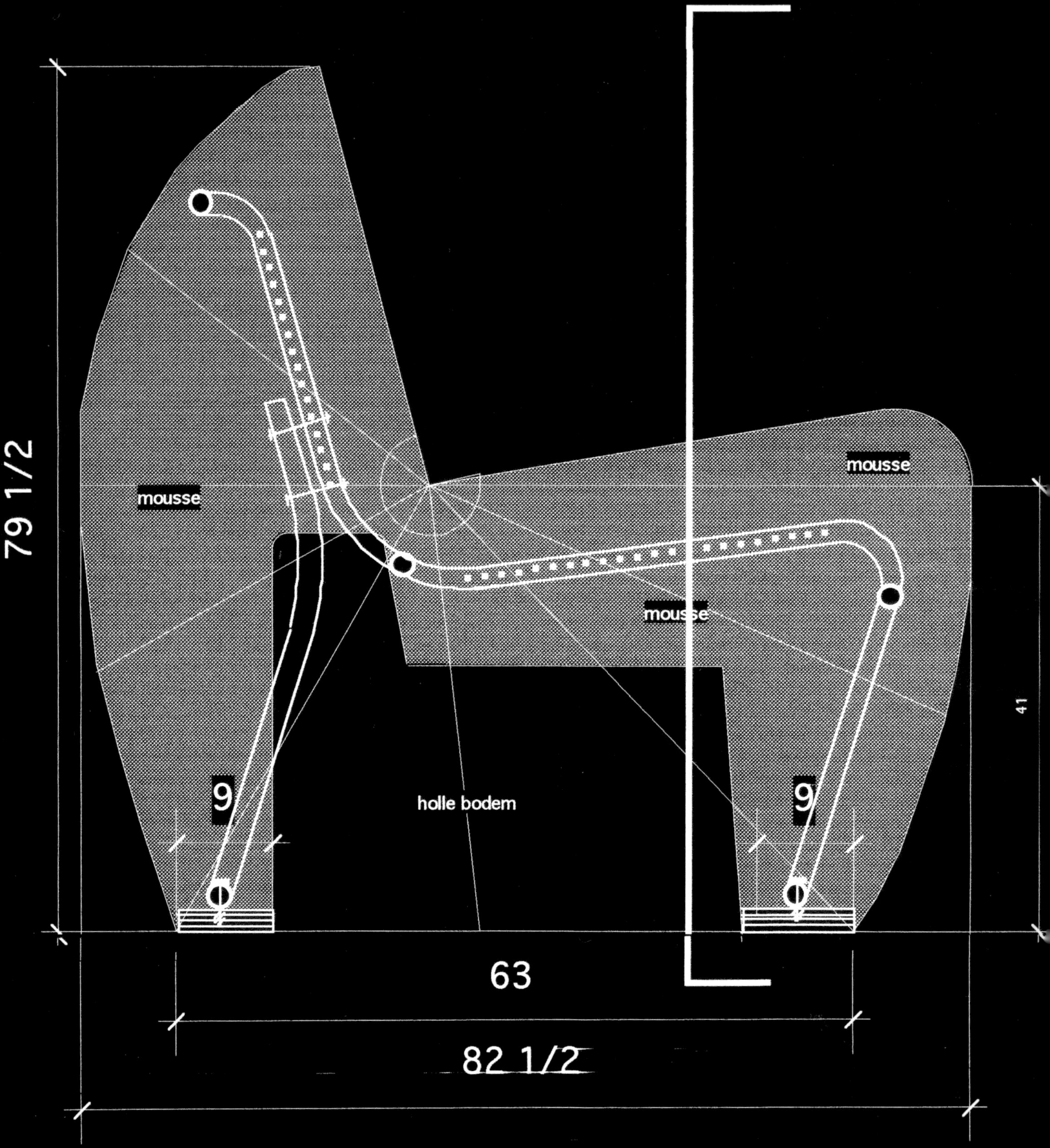

79 1/2
mousse
mousse
mousse
9
9
holle bodem
41
63
82 1/2

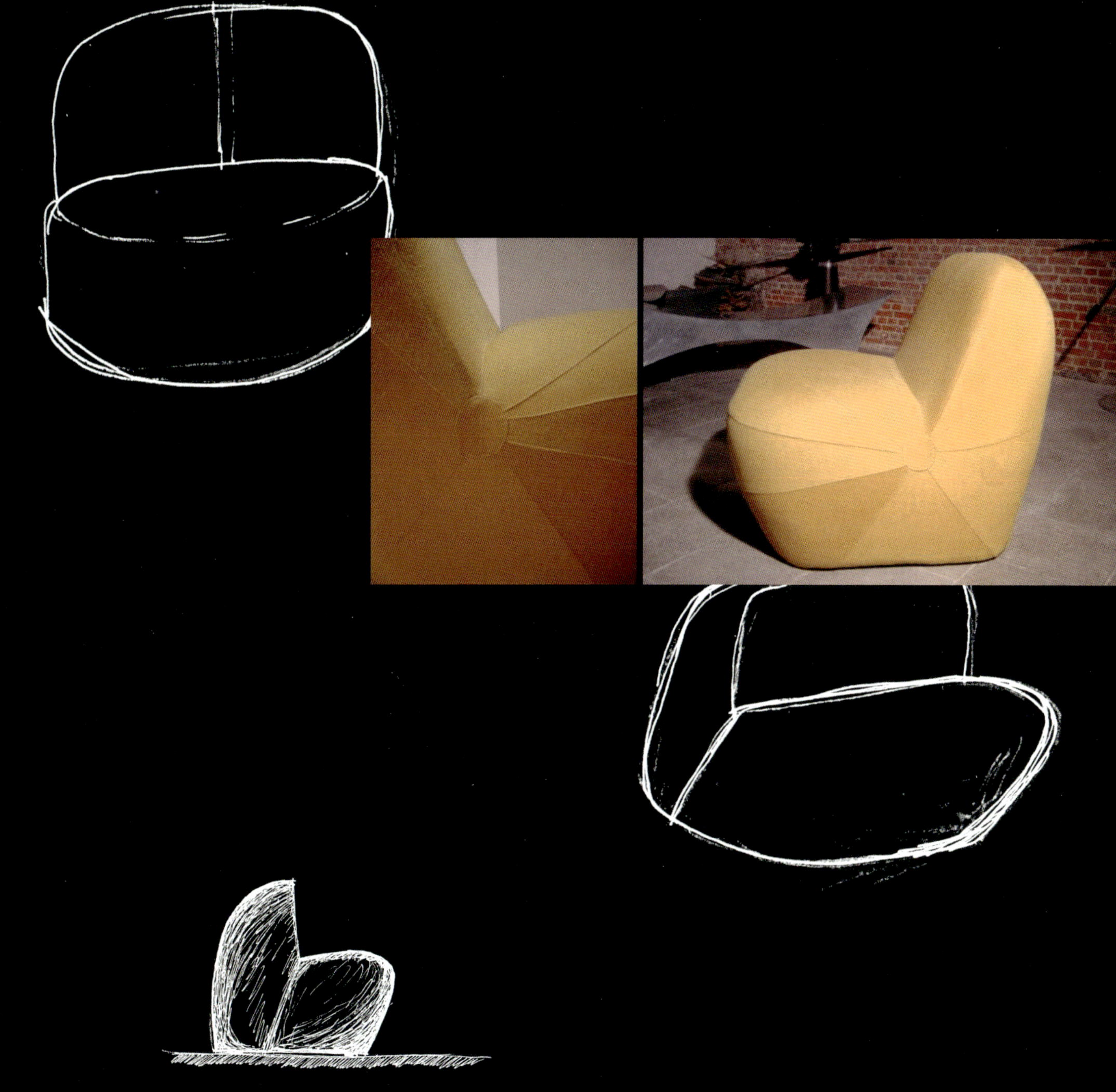

EMPEROR'S HAT, 1992 – "This prototype of a lounge seat was inspired by the typical hat of a Japanese emperor and was part of my one-man show at the *Yuill Crowley Gallery*. The inside consists of injection-moulded polyurethane that is supported by a simple steel structure. The upholstery-technique was inspired by a fan. So once again: it is about rendering three-dimensionality to a two-dimensional surface. In doing so I was also looking for a way to give the seat a certain dynamic, creating the illusion of movement."

VITEO

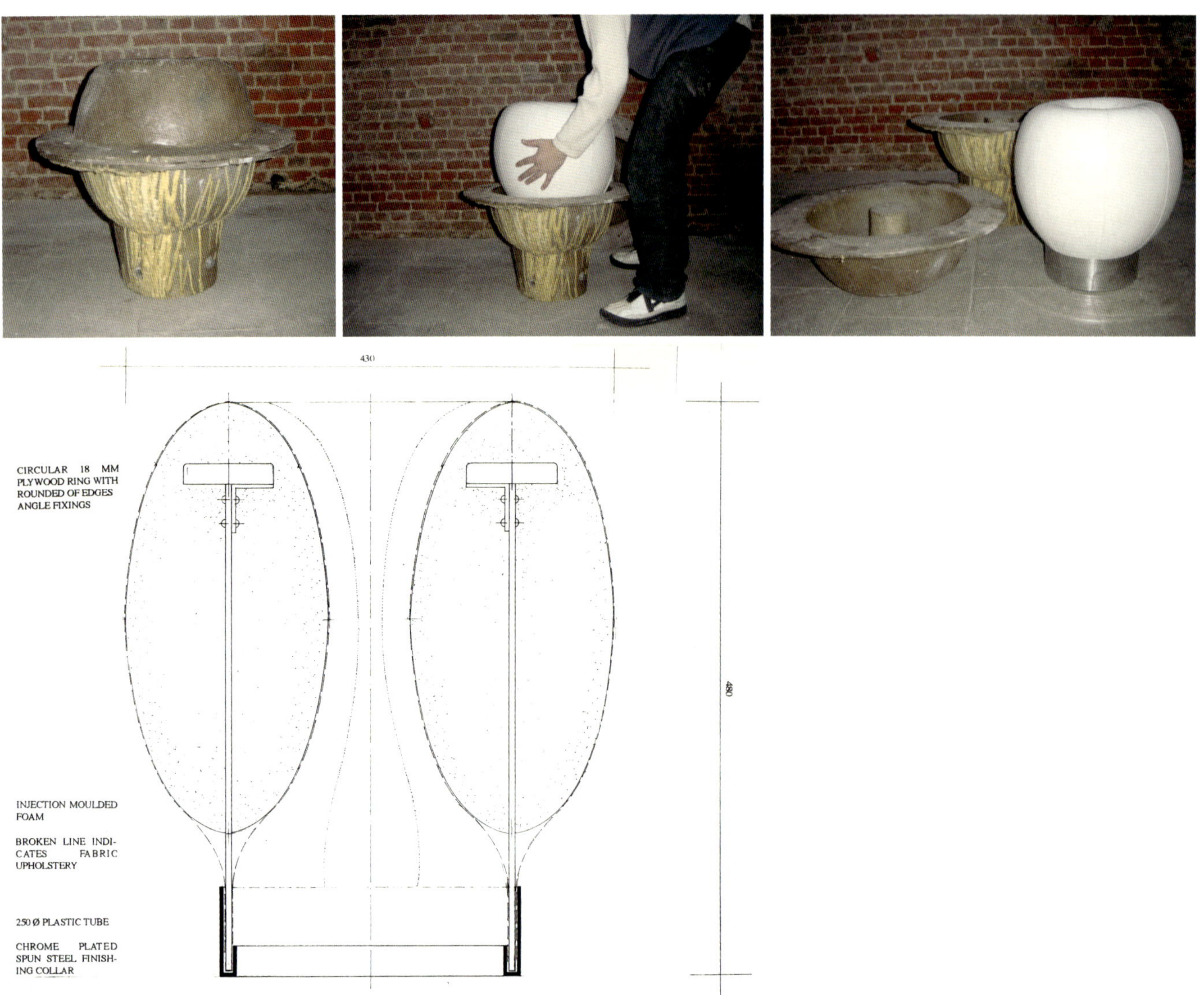

Q STOOL, 1990 – "When I started to do interiors, I soon discovered that the market didn't always offer what I was looking for. The Australian market is small, and there are few producers, while foreign furniture is rare and expensive, because of the transport and duty costs. And anyway: I've never wanted to be just a stylist living on other people's ideas. Australia has a lot of backyard industries working on a small scale, something that is much harder to find in Europe. The *Q stool* obtained its name from the *Q bar* in Sydney, for which it was originally designed. While the final result is time and again associated with a turban and the sultriness of Arabian Nights, its form was almost exclusively defined by the desire to create a piece of furniture that would be practical, solid and innovative – of use in lounges and other public spaces. It is in one piece and has no backrest, allowing the user to turn smoothly on its axis. The structure doesn't have any mechanical joints, which enhances its solidness. Low to the ground, it's an easy seat to carry around. You simply have to put your hand in the hole and pick it up. But above all, it's safe and practically harmless, which is not without importance in nightclubs. Because of its weight and softness, it's not at all a handy tool to beat someone up with. It's only later that you discover that a design like this has stylistically a lot in common with the rest of your work. In this case, the production technique of the *Q stool* is close to that of the *Burdekin barstool,* and based on what I would like to describe as a 'circular construction principle'. The inside consists of injection-moulded foam, supported by a steel tube. It's built around a hollow form. Because of this hole, many think it is an uncomfortable piece of furniture. But it's rather the contrary. You only need a support for both buttocks when you sit, not the whole surface. Of course, its design reminds people of a toilet, so it makes them laugh. But that's ok for me. As long as there is interaction, you have achieved a lot. Over the years, I created several limited editions, but it would take until 2005 before the Austrian manufacturer Viteo made it part of its collection, and turned it into outdoor furniture."

LEAF, 2008 – "Seamlessness is essential to me,
in order to create 'strong objects' that surprise by their naturalness. This is the first of a totally new range of shade makers, developed
for *Umbrosa*.   The technical innovation remains entirely hidden behind the most natural form one can think of: a giant stem and leaf."

Q SYDNEY, 1994, Q ADELAIDE, 1994, Q MELBOURNE, 1997, bars, Australia – "From the very beginning my interior designs were constructed around objects that were especially designed for a project. In an otherwise minimalist and restrained approach, in which the space was reduced and stripped to an open plan with its bare essentials, the objects were meant to be strong signs characterising the space. Nothing should distract the viewer's attention from the object's quintessence. In a more general way, these objects were meant to function as a logo, providing the venue with a corporate identity. In Q Sydney, a bar on the third floor of three merged buildings in Oxford Street, dating from the beginning of the 20th century, the interior was mainly organised around two elements, or visual hubs, which I added to the otherwise empty space. The main element of the setting was the counter, an oval when seen from above, and a 9 m long volume sculpted from lightweight concrete blocks. Its curved lines and fluid surfaces have later been associated with images of a marine world: from the keel of a ship to a polished pebble. I felt honoured, but in fact, its profile was mainly inspired by the postures clients take when hanging around and leaning on the counter top. While the refrigeration and stock were integrated in the block, I also created the possibility for clients to stand behind the bar next to the barman, knowing very well that only regulars would take advantage of this privilege. Even without the physical barrier, customers had to feel it was still there psychologically. It also created a round table effect, in which clients were not next to but facing each other. Stools – the second element – punctuated the space with a decisive note of colour. It was only after the success of Q Sydney that the owner decided to create a series of identical bars in Adelaide and Melbourne. The architectural language of Q Sydney served as an example but each kept its own individuality. While the form of the bar in Adelaide was much more rigid, the one in Melbourne went for the opposite. As a complement to the sturdy rectangular bar in Adelaide, sculpted in Y-tong blocs, the legs of three-penny-a-piece children's chairs were heightened with tubes to create delicate bar stools. In Melbourne, the Q identity had to be added to the already existing and daring interior by the Australian designer Tom Kovak. I built a long curved bar that swung through the large open space like a giant spermatozoid, its tail ending on the dancefloor, creating a booth for the deejay. Again the clients could sit and stand on both sides of the bar. Regular clients could even leave their bottles in personalised safe-deposit boxes."

STRAWS, 2009 – "Much more than just a lighting object, Straws is a totally new architectural lighting system, developed for Dark. The light is channelled through innumerable small tunnels, creating a unique poetic effect that is not unlike a snowy carpet of crystals. "

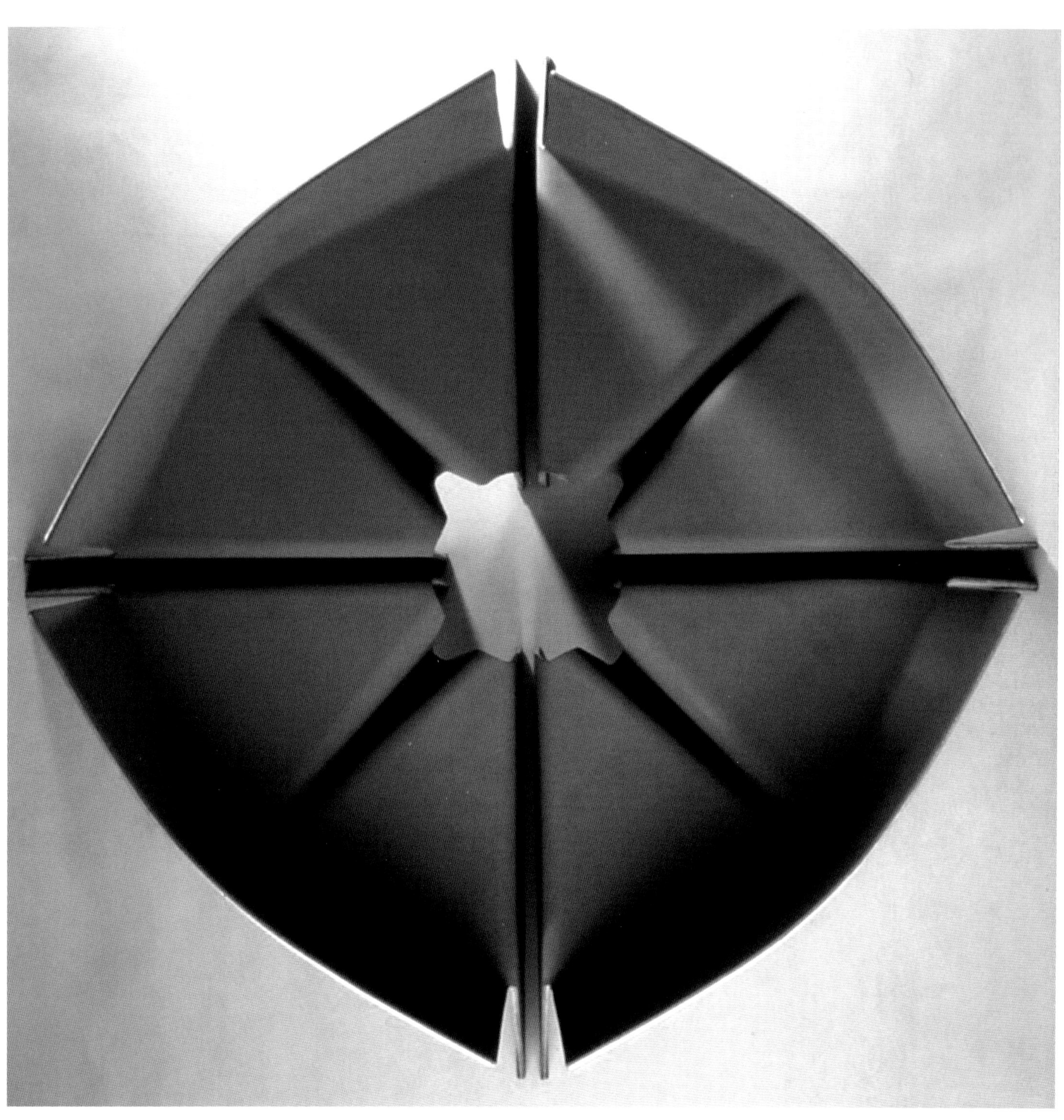

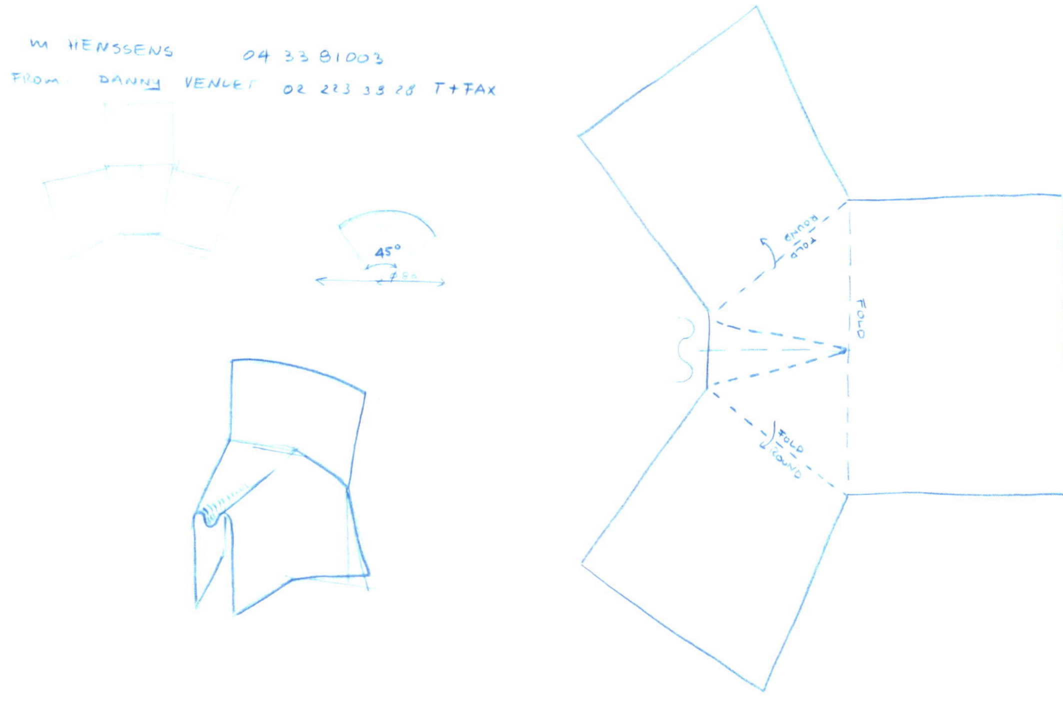

CAKE, 1998 – "To me, minimalism is not just a formal principle. It is above all a way of making life easier and simpler. *Cake* is extremely simple in its complexity. It is a block that unfolds in five objects. It grew out of an effort to eliminate the clutter caused by the numerous legs in the classic combination of a table and chairs. The four chairs can be moved entirely under the table top, like wedges of a cake. Hence the name. Its minimalism resides in the fact that the chairs of this prototype are folded origami-like from a single 3 mm sheet of aluminium curved to provide the chair with the necessary strength. The circular top is generated from the octagonal form produced by the backs of the gathered chairs. The chairs can also be stacked. Moulded plywood or plastic can be used as alternatives for fabrication."

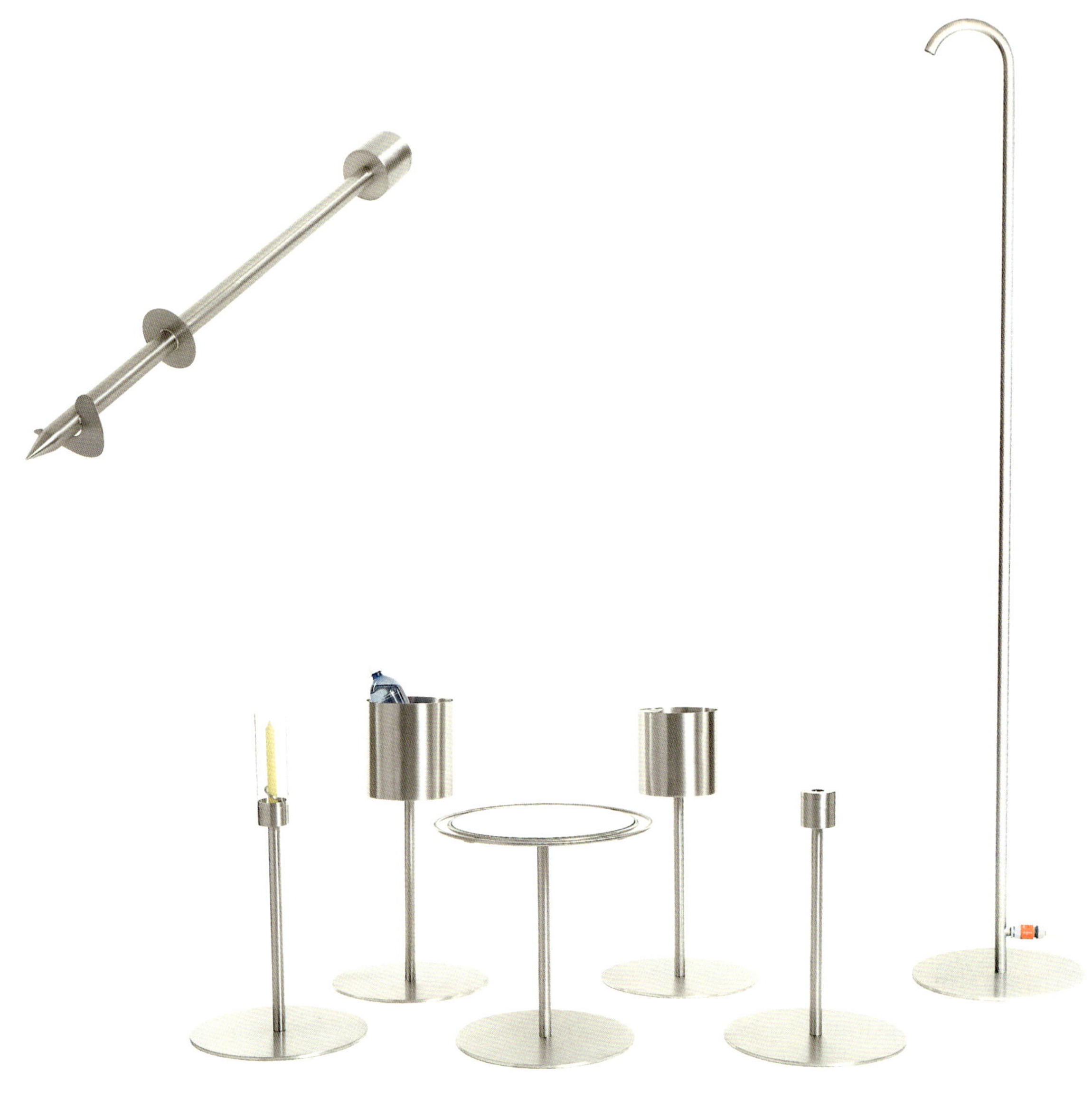

CAGES AUX FOLLES, 2007 – "*EI* was a project in which 12 Dutch and Belgian designers and artists were invited for a month's stay in Beijing, China, to work with Chinese artisans and return with some new products. *EI* stood for 'Entity/Identity', but it is also the Dutch word for 'egg', the form I ended up with when I decided to make a birdcage, in collaboration with the Yin Sum atelier, a workshop that normally produces kites. We created three cages of which two in stainless steel and one in bamboo strips. One stands upright; the two others lie on their side. I tried to create an object that would unite the many functions of the cage into one seamless design. In each of the cages the curvy lattice organically bulges inwards, creating two 'implosions'. The first bulge – long and tiny – is an alternative for the traditional stick on which the birds sits and rests. The second – short and wide – offers ample space for an arm to access the birdcage, while it also serves as a pedestal for a broken but precious piece of ceramic that closes the cavity, so that the birds can't escape. The ceramic fragments are an ode to Chinese tradition that still cultivates the imperfect, the weather-beaten and broken as exceptional qualities – in great contrast to our vision on design. Two cultures – east and west, old and new – have been confronted and brought together in harmony in one single object. However, it is the old and broken piece of ceramic that is put on a pedestal."

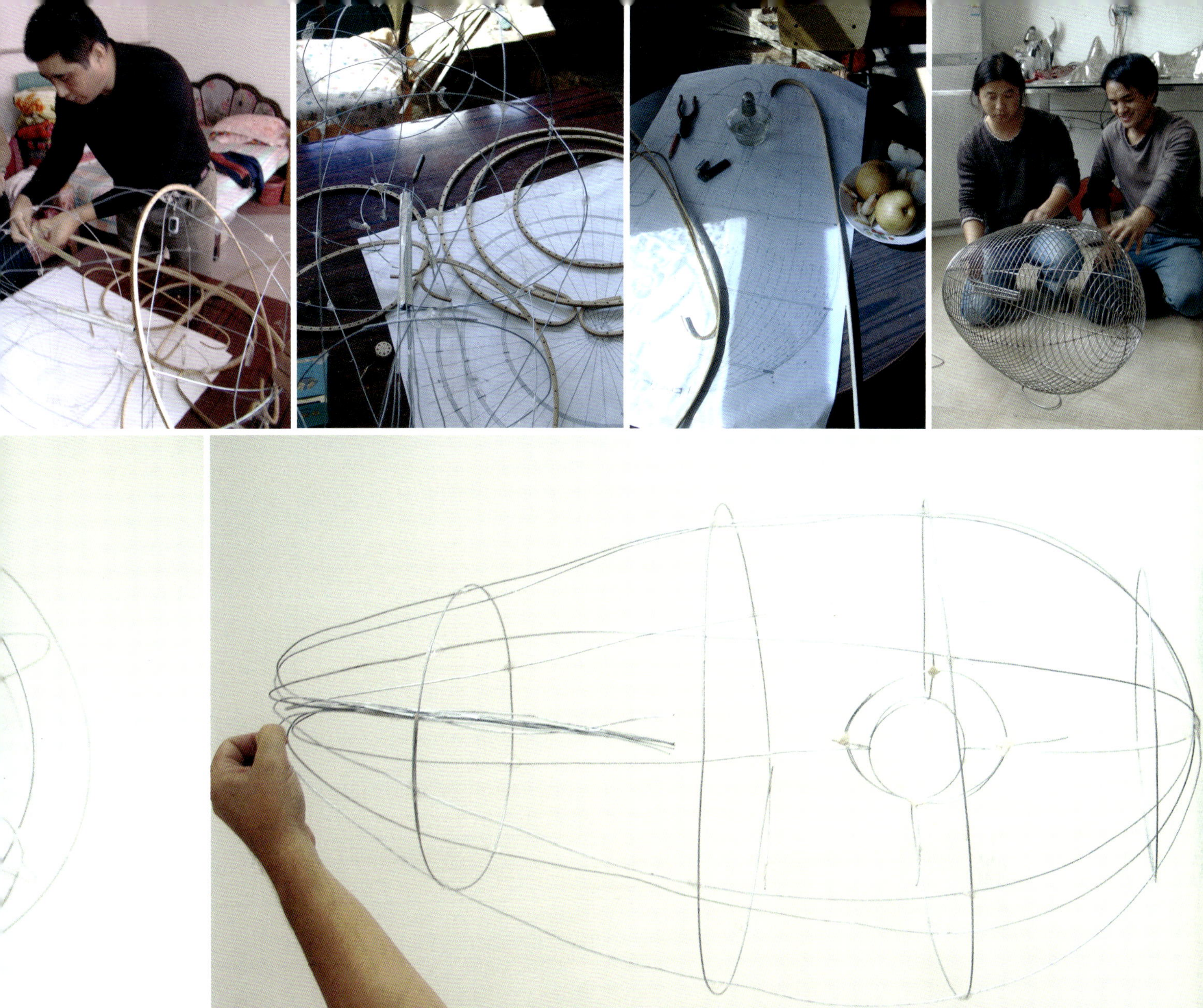

JEWEL STICKS, 2007 – "Not only the harmonising of Eastern and Western culture and the Old and New stood central in *Jewel Sticks*, the second series of limited editions I designed in China, as part of the *El*-project. It was also an effort to transform the most common everyday object, chopsticks, into something extremely precious and exclusive: a jewel. The collection comprises three pairs of chopsticks of which two are entirely in silver whereas the third one is a wood and silver combination. In the first two pairs, the part of the stick that lies in the hand has been redesigned in such a way that it perfectly encloses the top of the forefinger, while the second has been given a larger and more comfortable support in the ball of the thumb. The extremely minimal Asian sticks almost become a stalk for an opulent jewel with a Chinese vegetable motif. In the third pair each stick has been linked to three double rings giving it a prosthesis-like character. In each of these rings the smaller circle is drawn over the stick, while the larger one slides over the forefinger or thumb, thus offering a better grip. The rings also have the advantage that they can be worn as a jewel without the sticks."

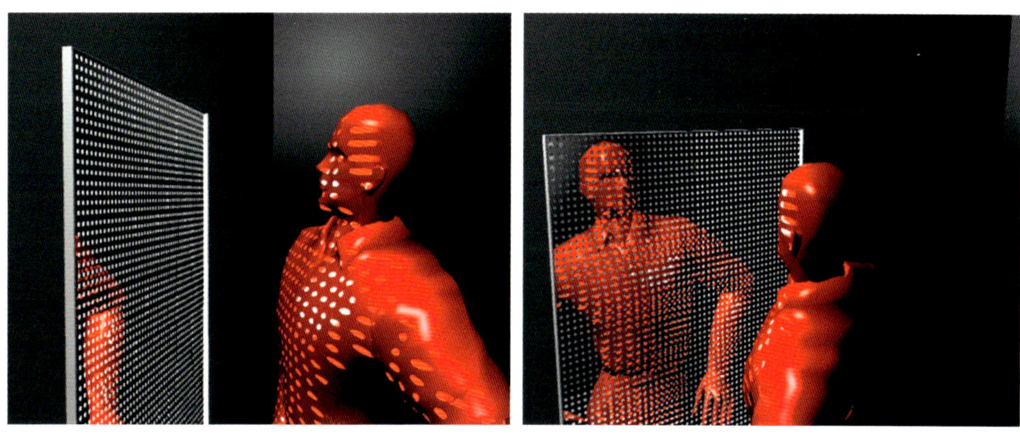

DOTS FOR REFLECT, 2002 – "I've often been compared to Dorian Gray, since I didn't seem to get any older. Those days are over now, but I still dislike mirrors. They confront you with too bitter a reality. They scare me. When the leading Belgian mirror manufacturer Deknudt-Decora invited me, Matali Crasset and a number of other designers to create a new collection of mirrors, Reflect!, I came up with an idea that expressed this horror and at the same time tried to temper the hard and implacable image. The surface of my mirror is pierced with a regular grid of small holes and lit from behind by a Led light-source. What remains is an image in pixels, very pop, like small polka dots. You can switch the light off when you look at yourself and vice versa. The pixels soften the traces of fatigue and age, while the daily confrontation also forces you to 'reflect' on your reflection – since the mirror makes it very clear that we always have to glue these pixels together to come to a whole, a vision that remains an illusion and is never real."

DELVAUX INSIDE-OUT, 2004 – "A famous Belgian manufacturer
of handbags and other leather accessories, Delvaux, celebrated its 175th anniversary. An equal number of artists were therefore asked
to do something with one of their products. The results would be compiled in a book. I started from a double idea. First: a handbag is
something to show off. And second: you never find something in a bag when you need it. So I proposed to create an inverted handbag:
with all the objects that are normally inside the bag, attached to the outside. In this one-off the objects were simply covered with a coating."

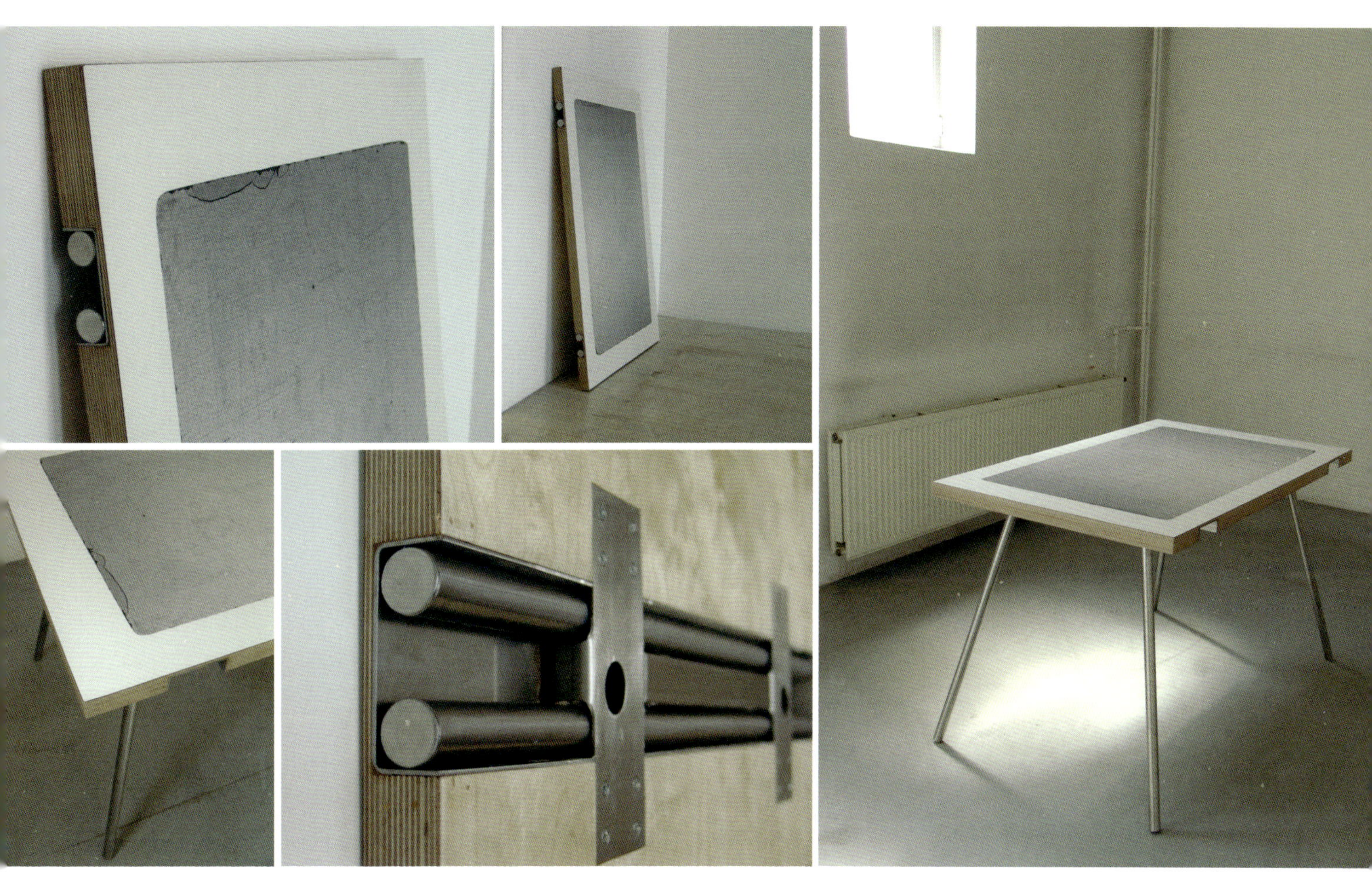

DOUBLE-TAKE-TABLE, 2001, Gallery Archetype, Brussels, Belgium, 2005 Künstlerbrüder, Haus der Kunst, Munich, Germany – "When I design an object for my own pleasure and not in function of a specific architectural project, the result is always closer to art than design. Despite the fact that these objects often serve as a source of inspiration for commercial products later on, they invariably also have the look and feel of a sculpture and statement. That's why I always gladly accept commissions that come from art galleries. In that sense the *Double-Take-Table*, which was created for the Brussels based Gallery Archetype, is certainly not an oddball in my work. That it looks different may be explained by the fact that I created it together with my brother Richard, who's six years younger, and a very successful artist. Central to this table is the idea of 'objet trouvé' and 'ready- made' that also plays an important role in the rest of his work. The object is an abstraction and remake of an ordinary kitchen table that we found in the street where I live. It has a tabletop that is made of 4 cm thick birch multiplex, coated with a Formica layer by Abet Laminati. Its stainless steel legs are completely removable by pushing them into the negative U-shaped frame at the back of the tabletop. Without legs the simple table becomes a precious artwork, which can be hung on a wall, drawing the attention to the print on its surface. The image shows the top of the old discarded table that served as a model, heavily eroded by time and its users, contrasting sharply with the new and still immaculate tabletop on which it is printed. The name of the object, which is synonymous to 'copy and paste', refers to the double function of the object as well as to its production technique. It is again about a game of contrasts that tries to bestow the viewer with feelings of surprise, pleasure, uncertainty and uneasiness. And in a way it also contains a criticism on design: everyone loves a picture of an old woman, while an old table is discarded. As to the difference between art and design: the table was produced in a limited edition of 12. For me it was the most expensive piece of furniture I ever created, for Richard it was cheapest piece of art. Need I say more?"

CARMAUSOLEUM, installation, 2006, Family Affairs exhibition, Bozar, Belgium. – "My brother Richard and I were separated several times during our youth, because of the roaming of our family and a divorce, but we always remained pretty close. As an artist he's not forced to come up with a solution with every new project: holding a mirror to the public can be enough. But *Carmausoleum*, another project that we did together, in collaboration with another duo from the arts world, the brothers Erik & Harald Thys, comes pretty close to a real solution to a real problem. The installation was created for *Family Affairs*, an exhibition that focused on brothers and sisters in art, from early history till today. The car serves as a backdrop and platform for some of the most important episodes in our lives. As a result, many have a close emotional bond with their car that is comparable to that of a family member. And yet: there's no graveyard where we can preserve and visit them, once they're out of function. Cars are a typical victim of consumer society. We therefore proposed a model for a *Carmausoleum*, where one would be able to stock his beloved car, in concrete niches that measured 5 by 3,4 and 2 m. The niches would be stacked on top of each other, creating a giant wall or monument, preferably in natural surroundings, next to a river or on a meadow. It could expand endlessly and soon take up the size of a suburb, while all niches would be open at both ends so that the cars would be clearly visible. Improbable as it may seem, I developed the plan up to the smallest detail. And that's where I feel the difference between Richard and me. He's happy with the concept, but I can't undo myself from the desire to see it in real life."

ARCHETYPE, temporary stand at the ArtBrussels art fair, 2001 – "I have this strategy: when you want to grab visitors by the neck at an event and make them interact, you first have to make them sit down and relax. That's why I created a bench along the walls of this stand at ArtBrussels. The booth also needed a storeroom. Instead of building it on the side, I put it in the middle, a manoeuvre that also provided more hanging surface. On one wall of the storeroom I integrated a row of computer screens, with a rather strange and 'negative' bench underneath. It was tempting to crawl in, but difficult to get out. So the people had the tendency to stay a bit longer, while the bench created a nice visual effect – as if the box was challenging gravity. The fluo-graffiti were by Belgian artist Jean-Luc Moerman, with whom I collaborated in a series of other projects, before he became world-famous."

FLANDERS DESIGN ICONS —ICONEN VAN DESIGN IN VLAANDEREN, exhibition architecture, 2003, Flemish Parliament, Brussels, Belgium – "This exhibition did not only show a series of design products of Flemish origin that had more or less acquired iconic status over the last fifteen years, or would most probably do so in the nearby future. It was also the first of a series of exhibitions that put the beauty of the recently restored and heritage listed counter hall of the former Brussels Postcheque building in evidence, in which the exhibition was organised. Moreover, the exhibition had to draw the attention to its new function. Part of the administration and logistics of the Parliament of the Flemish community in Belgium had recently moved to the Postcheque building, built after World War II by the Belgian modernist architect Victor Bourgeois, and the counter hall that was on the ground floor of this fantastic landmark, was to be at the centre of the new Open-House politics, with which the Parliament of the Flemish community in Belgium wanted to make itself better known, while also promoting the Flemish identity in general. We won the competition for the scenography of the exhibition with a humble and simple plan that tried to enforce the most impressive symmetric architecture of the counter hall, instead of going against it. We also had set ourselves the task to create a neutral backdrop for objects that had been selected by a committee, comprising a heterogeneous mix of furniture, cars, suitcases, electronic devices, accessories, glass, silver, ceramics, textile and graphic design. So we started with the idea of a box in a box, but kept the box low, at shoulder height, and eliminated its ceiling so that the visitors would at all times have an overview of the counter hall. Painted in a neutral white, the box was traversed by a crisscross of straight corridors that divided the exhibition into a number of smaller platforms, on which one or a small ensemble of objects was shown. The result was a labyrinth that on the one hand underlined the symmetric grid of the hall with its basic chessboard pattern and rigid architecture, and on the other playfully broke through that pattern with a Mikado of corridors, never offering a general overview of the objects on show."

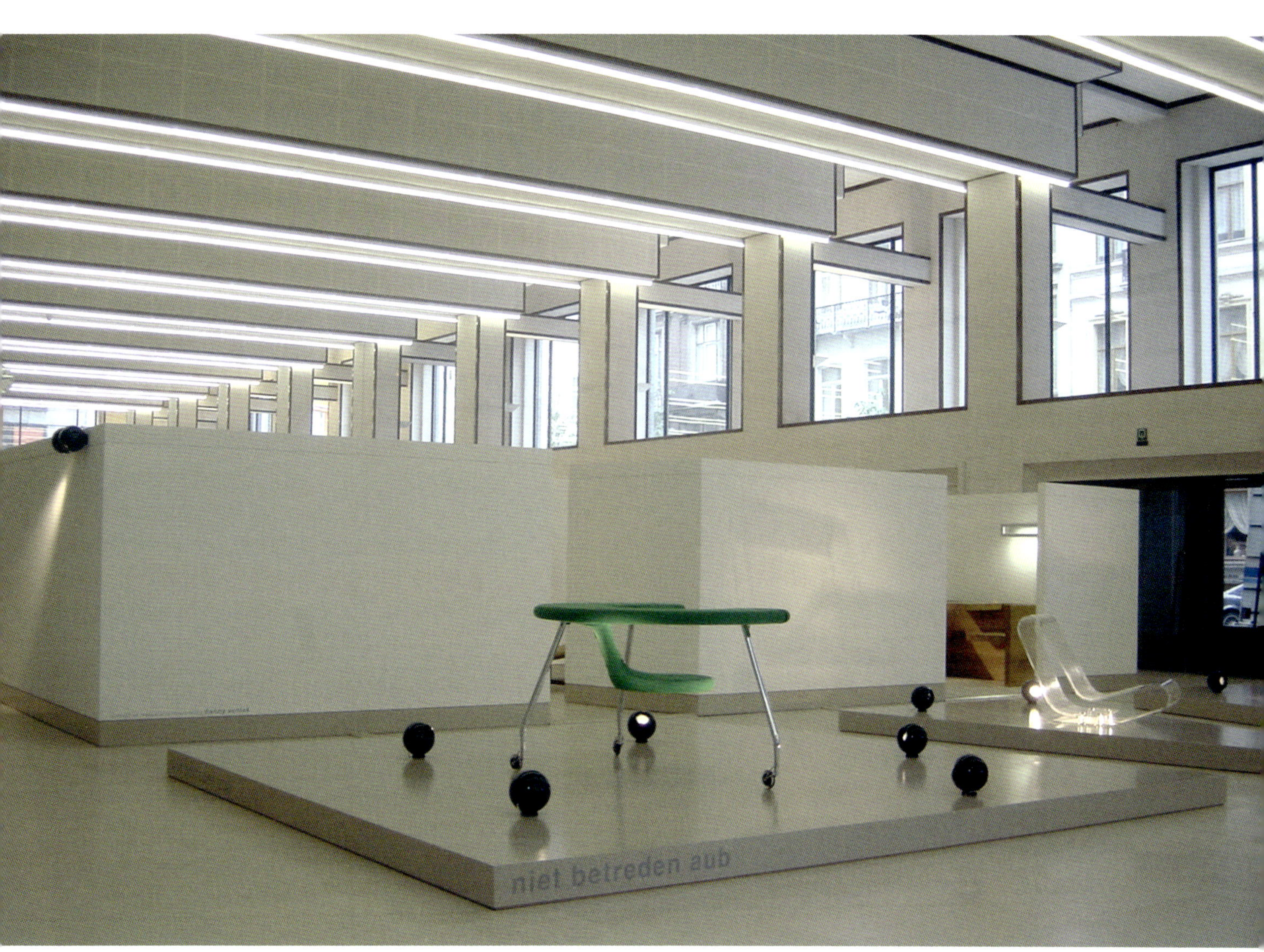

niet betreden aub

ICI ET MAINTENANT, Bar, lounge and meeting point, 2001, Thurn & Taxis, Brussels, Belgium – "A huge space in one of the main buildings of a famous and historically very valuable industrial site in Brussels, in disuse and to be renovated at the time of the exhibition, had to be temporarily transformed into a bar, lounge and meeting point, for a group show of contemporary art: *Ici et Maintenant*, an inititiative of Laurent Jacob. I had to use the chipboard that was provided by way of sponsorship, not exactly the ideal material when you think of a lounge. Starting from the tight and repetitive grid of the oversized columns that structured the immense and bare hall, I created a modular landscape by cladding these vertical beams with the chipboard and connecting their ends below and above with horizontal beams, that served as a seating element at ground level. The result was that these modules were not lost in space, but became part of a portal, framing the seated visitors as in a series of *tableaux vivants*. The decoration was left to a friend of mine, the young graffiti artist Luc Moerman. His grungy approach perfectly fitted the design."

TRANSIT, exhibition architecture, 2001, Brussels, Belgium –
"*Transit* was the first major design event in Brussels, with a series of exhibitions spread all over town. I assisted the artistic director, Max Borka, as the event's architect, which allowed me to develop some typical exhibition furniture, such as the giant counter in *Things to Come* and a equally giant platform in which ceramic pieces were shown under ready-made curvy acrylic domes."

DESIGNDOCTORS, designers collective, a collaboration with Dirk Meylaerts, Olivier Gilson en Ronald Mattelé, 2001-2002, Belgium – "When the time came to decide on a profession, I was initially interested in architecture but had no idea what this involved. It was my father who advised me to study medicine. I didn't really have to be convinced: already as a boy I dreamed of becoming a doctor or a cook. It was probably a good thing for humanity that I didn't become either. When I started studying medicine it was all about chemistry, physics and pills. Man himself didn't really seem all that important. So I stopped. But my attitude as a designer is still very similar to that of a doctor. What drives me is a passion and fascination for men – their habits, rituals, attitudes and psychology. Man is my primal material. I observe. How do they move? How do they function? I want to influence their interaction with objects and environments. Or make them think and experience space with a new intensity and awareness. Any design that doesn't have this social ambition is pure decoration, or passes over the people's heads. Together with three other protagonists of the Brussels design world – Dirk Meylaerts, Ronald Mattelé and Olivier Gilson – I launched in 2000 the *DesignDoctors*, as part of Transit, a design route through Brussels. It was an experiment in democratic design, with the Red Cross as our logo. People could visit our temporary shop and ask for a diagnosis of a problem they had with their interior, while they were charged no more than they would pay for a visit to the doctor. The prescription that resulted was free of obligation but could eventually lead to further 'treatment'. We kept on doing this during other events, but the initiative was so successful that we finally had to abandon the project. We started to feel like *Do-It-Yourself-Doctors* and were mostly consulted for problems that had little to do with the fundamentals of design. Nevertheless: the dream is still there to give it a sequel."

ICECUBE, 2002 – "There are many times I wish design could always be this easy. When we needed an ice cooler in the *DesignDoctors'* stand at the Interieur Biennale in Kortrijk, I designed a white container in rotation moulded polyethylene that looks like a giant ice-cube shining in the dark. The two blacklights placed underneath the cube evoke coolness and freshness. By simply turning the container upside down and because of two different depths it can be used for differently sized bottles,. An optional tray provides additional space for glasses. The *IceCube* serves as a beacon, a space divider, a meeting point and a party enhancer. It is part of the Extremis collection and has become one my most successful designs".

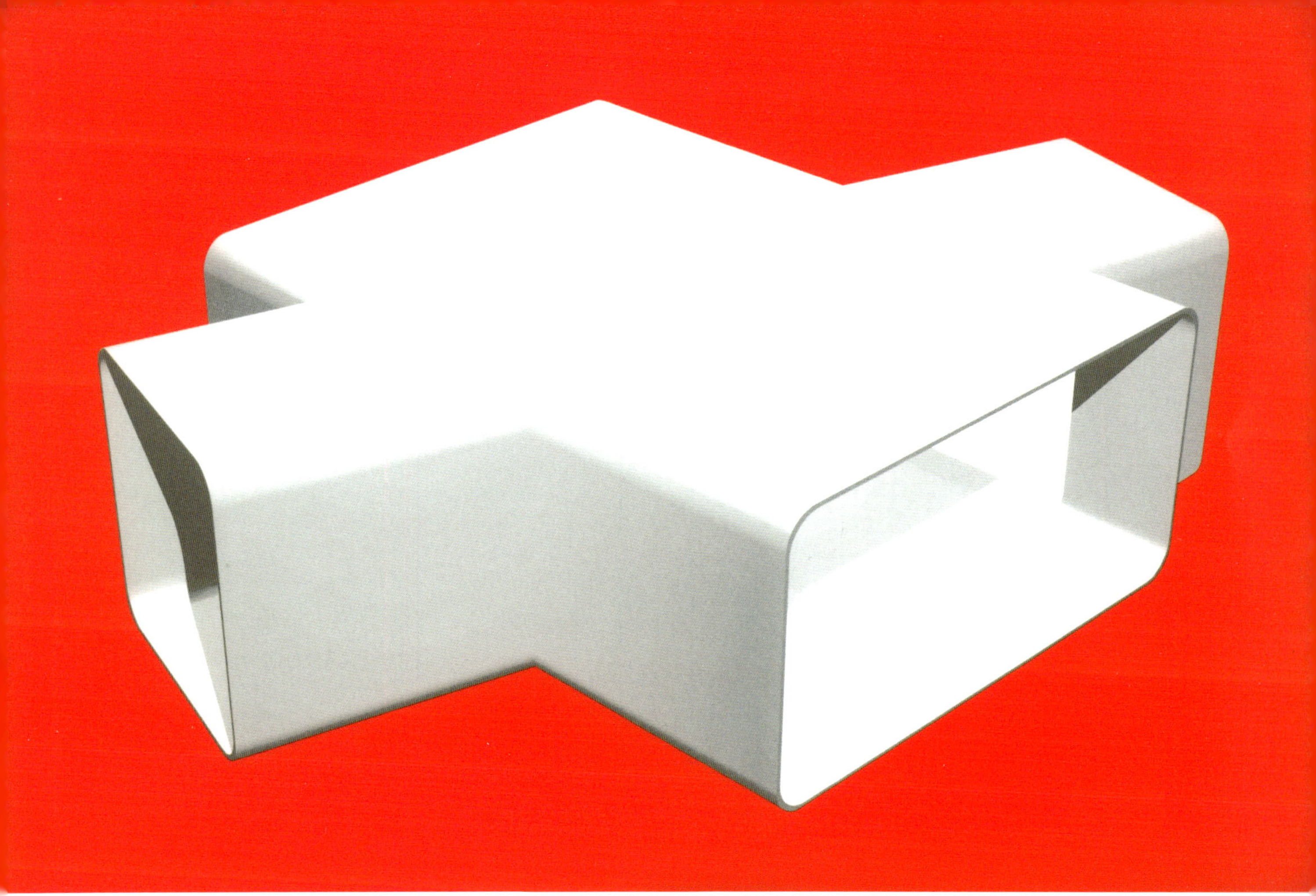

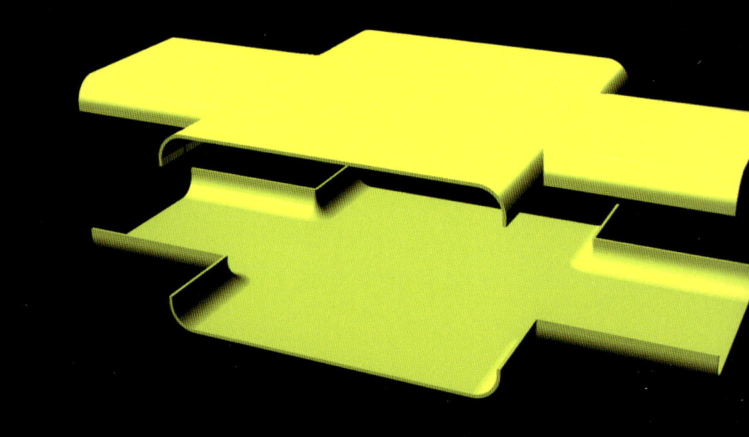

BRUSSELS DESIGN DISTRICT / DESIGNBRUSSELS, logo and architectural element, 2003/2005, Brussels, Belgium – "The logo for the *designbrussels* event, a three-dimensional box or can, grew out of an architectural element in the form of a cross that had been part of the plans for the *Brussels Design District* (BDD), two years earlier. BDD was meant to become a giant and permanent platform for design, starting with one floor of 40000 m² in the Brussels Trade Mart complex, near the Atomium, as an initiative of the American Tramwell Crow group. The architectural element had to link the corridors, while its form partly referred to the cross-pollination between all thinkable fields in design, key to BDD's politics."

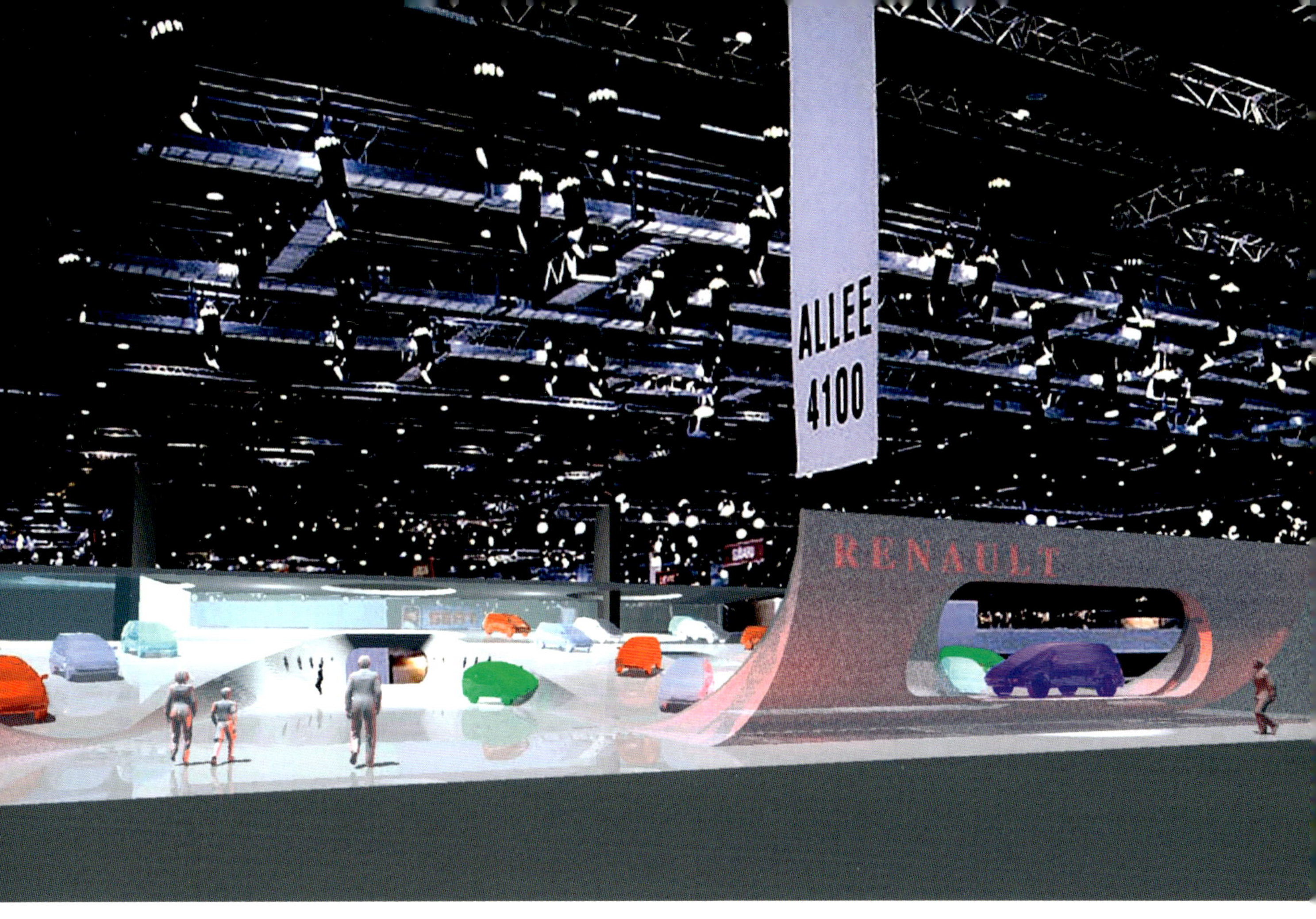

ALLEE
4100
RENAULT

RED CROSS ASYLUM, exhibition architecture, 2005, Brussels, Belgium — "This traveling exhibition, an initiative of Red Cross, was mainly aimed at youngsters. It introduced them to the specific problems of asylum seekers and the twisting path they have to follow. Hence the mobile and modular benches in foam, that can be combined into various zigzagging patterns, to fit the demands of the different spaces where the exhibition would be shown. The exhibition elements, developed together with Album, served as a link between the benches. The lowness of the benches literally forced the visitors to sit down in order to play interactive games, since I absolutely wanted to avoid an academic atmosphere. I wanted them to relax, play, reflect, meditate, discuss and dialogue."

vict
LE JOURNAL
France est un pays fragile dirigé par les
res qui ont renversé l'Ancien Régime quatre
Menacée par les pays voisins, qui voient d'un
ce nouvel Etat, la république française
mes.
Loin de Paris
où la populat
la répression
Le représen
Jean-Baptist
ordonne un
d'exécution
principale
dans la Lo
macabre é
scène. De
hellmann

1988

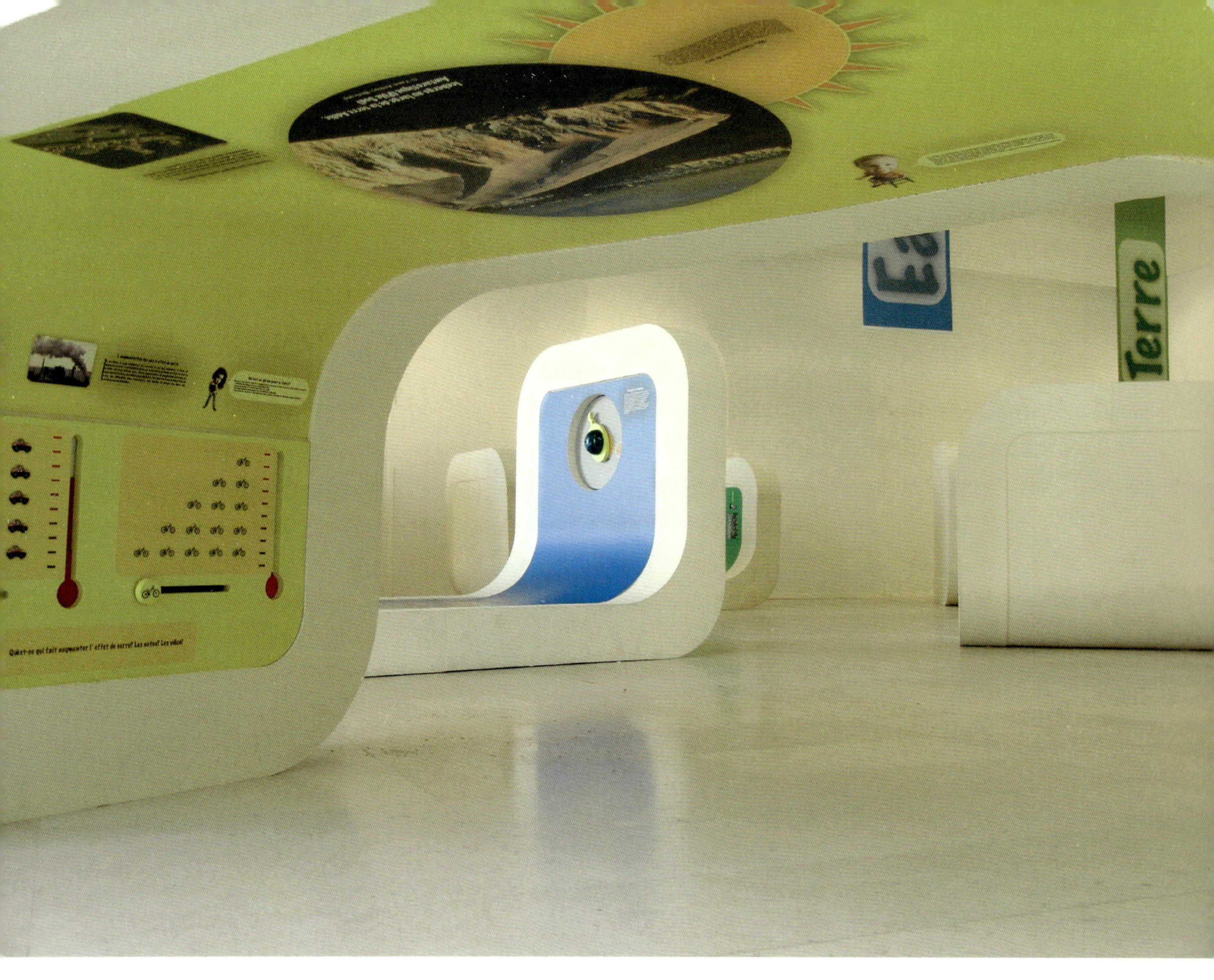

QUAND LA NATURE S'EN MELE, exhibition architecture, 2005, St Jean de Monts, France – "This project was the result of a collaboration with Olivier Guilbaud of Album, with whom we also developed the Red Cross exhibitions, and Thierry Lahaye. The exhibition was part of a local festival for children and explained the natural biotope of a French seaside village, seen in a global perspective. The approach was very playful and touched questions such as: Why do birds migrate? Who gives the sign for take-off? And so on. The presentation was built around three elements: sun, sea and land. When these objects referred to the sea, the module was blue and lying on its back, like a boat. When sun was the subject, the elements were yellow and placed in a reversed position, like a table with the exhibition elements under it. Finally, the elements that referred to the earth were shown in an upright position and coloured green. The scenography was realised with nine modules in U-form cut out of three blocks of foam that served as a support for the objects on display. An old Australian game had inspired me to cut the elements in the most economical way. Out of one block we cut three U's that fitted into each other. With what was left we created children's furniture. It was a soft exhibition, allowing the children to hang around, sit, lie down and relax – without any risk of being hurt. The exhibition had a record number of visitors."

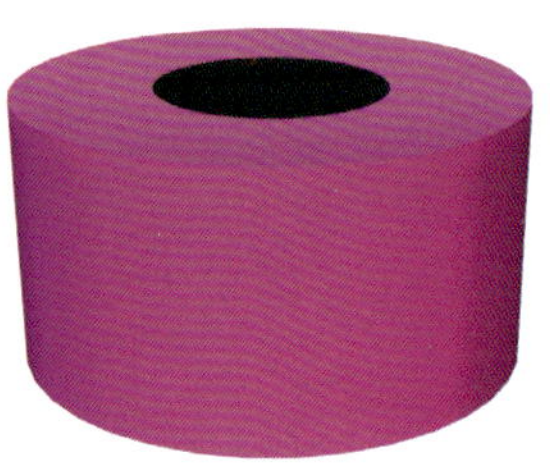

LET's DROP, 2004, Belgium – "I have the right to say: Ceci n'est pas du design. It is a non-design. I simply took my favorite candies, Liquorice All Sorts, dropjes in Dutch, and enlarged them to the size of furniture pieces: *Sandwiched, Twisted, 2 Tired, Rock'n roll, Cute Cube, Bric à Brac and Disc'oh*. Together they make *The original children's Furniture Allsorts* collection. It may remind some of the Sgt. Pepper's Lonely Hearts Club Band. Rightly so: it's probably the closest thing to Pop that I've ever done. Born from a contribution to a special issue of AddictLab magazine on 'fun', this collection of poufs was later taken into production by MNM Lifestyle Solutions. Made from polyester foam with polyurethane coating, they were originally meant for children, but are also a big success with adults."

ILLY LOUNGE , temporary lounge, 2004, ArtBrussels arts fair, Brussels, Belgium – "I've often been called the world's most laidback designer and I must admit: most of my designs, be it the umpteenth lounge, a sofa, a shower, or a massage centre, have something to do with relaxing. The coffee brand Illy asked me and my friend and colleague Dirk Meylaerts to set up a lounge at the Brussels arts fair, where people could drink coffee and relax. The collision of contrasting ideas such as relaxing on the one hand, and coffee which is meant to wake you up on the other hand, brought us to a Sunday breakfast in bed. A limited budget led us to a non-design, based on 'objets trouvés' or found objects. We simply drove through Brussels, picked up some abandoned mattresses, and coated them in elastic polyurethane, the sort of material used to waterproof roofs. It sealed the mattresses in a sexy, violent and glamorous red, which were then loosely spread on the floor. The soft red light of Dark's *No Fruit* lights made the Illy lounge complete."